A MOST USEFUL BOOK OF

FUNDAMENTALS OF PROGRAMMING LANGUAGES - I
(FPL I)
(CODE : 110003)

For
Semester I
First Year Degree Course in Engineering
Common for All Branches

As Per New Revised Syllabus of University of Pune
Effective from May 2013

Prof. Tulsidas R. Patil
M.E. (Comp)
Assistant Prof. I.T. Department
STES's NBN Sinhgad School of Engineering
Ambegaon, Pune

Prof. Madhuri A. Aher
M.Tech. (Comp)
Assistant Prof. Computer Department
STES's Sinhgad Academy of Engineering
Kondhwa (BK), Pune

Prof. Sonali T. Kadam
B.E. (Comp)
Lecturer Computer Department
SPVP's S.B. Patil College of Engineering
Vangali, Indapur. (Dist. Pune)

Prof. Apurva N. Varade
M.E. (Comp)
Assistant Prof. I.T. Department
STES's Sinhgad Academy of Engineering
Kondhwa (Bk), Pune

N 2760

FUNDAMENTALS OF PROGRAMMING LANGUAGES – I	ISBN NO. 978-93-83073-36-8
First Edition : August 2015	
© : Author	

The text of this publication, or any part thereof, should not be reproduced or transmitted in any form or stored in any computer storage system or device for distribution including photocopy, recording, taping or information retrieval system or reproduced on any disc, tape, perforated media or other information storage device etc., without the written permission of Author with whom the rights are reserved. Breach of this condition is liable for legal action.

Every effort has been made to avoid errors or omissions in this publication. In spite of this, errors may have crept in. Any mistake, error or discrepancy so noted and shall be brought to our notice shall be taken care of in the next edition. It is notified that neither the publisher nor the author or seller shall be responsible for any damage or loss of action to any one, of any kind, in any manner, therefrom.

Published By :	Printed By :
NIRALI PRAKASHAN	**REPRO INDIA LTD.**
Abhyudaya Pragati, 1312, Shivaji Nagar,	50/2, TTC/MIDC, Mahape,,
Off J.M. Road, PUNE – 411005	NAVI MUMBAI
Tel - (020) 25512336/37/39, Fax - (020) 25511379	Phone – (022) 27782011
Email : niralipune@pragationline.com	

DISTRIBUTION CENTRES

PUNE
Nirali Prakashan
119, Budhwar Peth, Jogeshwari Mandir Lane
Pune 411002, Maharashtra
Tel : (020) 2445 2044, 66022708
Fax : (020) 2445 1538
Email : bookorder@pragationline.com

MUMBAI
Nirali Prakashan
385, S.V.P. Road, Rasdhara Co-op. Hsg. Society Ltd.,
Girgaum, Mumbai 400004, Maharashtra
Tel : (022) 2385 6339 / 2386 9976,
Fax : (022) 2386 9976
Email : niralimumbai@pragationline.com

DISTRIBUTION BRANCHES

NAGPUR
Pratibha Book Distributors
Above Maratha Mandir, Shop No. 3, First Floor,
Rani Jhanshi Square, Sitabuldi, Nagpur 440012,
Maharashtra, Tel : (0712) 254 7129

HYDERABAD
Nirali Book House
22, Shyam Enclave, 4-5-947, Badi Chowdi
Hyderabad 500095, Andhra Pradesh
Tel : (040) 6554 5313, Mob : 94400 30608
Email : niralibooks@yahoo.com

CHENNAI
Pragati Books
9/1, Montieth Road, Behind Taas Mahal, Egmore,
Chennai 600008 Tamil Nadu, Tel : (044) 6518 3535,
Mob : 94440 01782 / 98450 21552 / 98805 82331
Email : bharatsavla@yahoo.com

JALGAON
Nirali Prakashan
34, V. V. Golani Market, Navi Peth, Jalgaon 425001,
Maharashtra, Tel : (0257) 222 0395
Mob : 94234 91860

KOLHAPUR
Nirali Prakashan
New Mahadvar Road,
Kedar Plaza, 1st Floor Opp. IDBI Bank
Kolhapur 416 012, Maharashtra. Mob : 9855046155

BENGALURU
Pragati Book House
House No. 1,Sanjeevappa Lane, Avenue Road Cross,
Opp. Rice Church, Bengaluru – 560002.
Tel : (080) 64513344, 64513355,
Mob : 9880582331, 9845021552
Email:bharatsavla@yahoo.com

RETAIL OUTLETS
PUNE

Pragati Book Centre
157, Budhwar Peth, Opp. Ratan Talkies,
Pune 411002, Maharashtra
Tel : (020) 2445 8887 / 6602 2707, Fax : (020) 2445 8887

Pragati Book Centre
Amber Chamber, 28/A, Budhwar Peth,
Appa Balwant Chowk, Pune : 411002, Maharashtra,
Tel : (020) 20240335 / 66281669
Email : pbcpune@pragationline.com

Pragati Book Centre
676/B, Budhwar Peth, Opp. Jogeshwari Mandir,
Pune 411002, Maharashtra
Tel : (020) 6601 7784 / 6602 0855

PBC Book Sellers and Stationers
152, Budhwar Peth, Pune 411002, Maharashtra
Tel : (020) 2445 2254 / 6609 2463

MUMBAI
Pragati Book Corner
Indira Niwas, 111 - A, Bhavani Shankar Road, Dadar (W), Mumbai 400028, Maharashtra
Tel : (022) 2422 3526 / 6662 5254
Email : pbcmumbai@pragationline.com

Dedicated to...

Our beloved parents for their unwavering faith, love and support.

... Authors

ACKNOWLEDGEMENT

Firstly we would like to extend our sincere thanks to the management (Sinhgad Technical Education Society and Shajirao Patil Vikas Pratishthan), also the Principal's and HOD's from NBN Sinhgad School of Engineering, Ambegaon, Sinhgad Academy of Engineering, Kondhawa (BK), and S. B. Patil College of Engineering, Vangali Indapur for their vital encouragement and support.

We also take this opportunity to express a deep sense of gratitude towards our colleagues namely Prof. Ranjeet Mote, Prof. Amol Dhumane, Prof. Laxmi Thakare, Prof. Bhushan Thakare and Prof. Nakul Sharma for their valuable information, constant encouragement and exemplary guidance, which helped us in completing this task through various stages.

Our special thanks to the publisher Mr. Dineshbhai Furia, Mr. Jignesh Furia and Mr. M. P. Munde and Mrs Deepali Lachake of Nirali Prakashan, Pune. We are also thankful to all the staff members of Nirali Prakashan for their constant efforts.

Most especially thanks to our beloved friends, relatives and family members for their blessings, help, guidance and best wishes.

We wish to express our profound thanks to all those who helped in making this book a reality and finally extend our heartfelt gratitude to all the students.

-**Authors**

PREFACE

Dear Students,

It gives us immense pleasure in introducing you about the First Edition of the book **'Fundamentals of Programming Language – I'**. This book strictly written as per the new revised syllabus of University of Pune.

This book is an attempt from the authors to cover all the topics of the entire syllabus of first semester as prescribed by University of Pune with simple and lucid explanations. Even teachers in this area would find this book helpful in introducing the concepts of Bharat Operating System, Algorithms and concepts of 'C' language.

This book is divided into four units.

In first two units, authors Madhuri Aher and Apurva Varade introduces you about the concepts of Open Source, Operating System, Various Programming Languages, Configuration of programming environment and Basics of Algorithm, which helps you in understanding the of popular programming languages and the open source operating system.

In third and forth unit authors Tulsidas Patil and Sonali Kadam focused the light on concepts of 'C' language, which helps you to learn the basics of 'C' programming language and acquire the art of computer programming.

We hope that this book will serve as a prelude to this exciting new syllabus of FPL-I.

Valuable suggestions from our esteemed readers to improve the book are most welcome and highly appreciated.

Authors

SYLLABUS

Teaching Scheme
Theory : 1 Hr/Week
Practicals : 2 Hrs /Week

Examination Scheme
On-Line : 50 Marks

Objectives
- To learn and acquire art of computer programming.
- To know about some popular programming languages and how to choose a programming language for solving a problem using a computer.
- To learn basics of programming in C

Unit	Syllabus	Hr
I	Introduction to Open Source Operating Systems and Programming Languages Introduction to Bharat Operating System (BOSS) GNU/Linux users model GUI, System Folders, study Commands (Using command terminal) with switches : Is, Directory Commands, Change user, privileges, passwords, tty, who, config, make, rpm, yum, sudo, Shutdown.	01
	Eclipse Editor, Compiler, Linker, Libraries, GUI, Configuring Programming Environments : C, C++. Java, Python (Pydev), Output, Debug windows	01
	Introduction to types of Programming Languages-Machine-level, Assembly-level and High-level Languages, Scripting Languages, Natural Languages; Their relative Advantages and Limitations. Characteristics of a Good Programming Language; Selecting a Language out of many available languages for coding an application; subprograms. Short Introduction to LISP, Simulation Platforms: MATLAB and GNU Octave(Open Source), Importance of Documentation, Documentation Platform LATEX (Free ware/Open Source).	02
II	Algorithm; Advantages of Generalized Algorithms; How to Make Algorithms Generalized; Avoiding Infinite Loops in Algorithms – By Counting, By using a Sentinel Value; Different ways of Representing an Algorithm – As a Program, As a Flowchart, As a Pseudo code; Need for Planning a Program before Coding; Program Planning Tools – Flowcharts, Structure charts, Pseudo codes;	01
	Importance of use of Indentation in Programming; Structured Programming Concepts – Need for Careful Use of "Go to" statements, How all programs can be written using Sequence Logic, Selection Logic and Iteration (or looping) Logic, functions.	01
III	Character set, Constants, Variables, keywords and Comments; Operators and Operator Precedence; Statements; I/O Operations; Preprocessor Directives; Pointers, Arrays and Strings; User Defined Data Types-Structure and Union;	03
IV	Control Structures-Conditional and Unconditional Branching Using "if", "switch", "break", "continue", "go to" and "return" Statements; Loop Structures – Creating Pretest Loops using "for" and "while" Statements; Creating Post test Loops using "do ... while" statement; Functions – Creating Subprograms using Functions; Parameter Passing by Value; Parameter Passing by Reference; Main Function with argv, argc[]. Definition of Testing and /Debugging	03

CONTENTS

1. Introduction   1.1 – 1.50

- 1.1 Introduction to Operating System   1.1
  - 1.1.1 Operating System   1.1
  - 1.1.2 Types of Operating System   1.2
- 1.2 Open Source   1.3
  - 1.2.1 Open-Source Software (OSS)   1.3
- 1.3 BOSS   1.3
  - 1.3.1 BOSS Features   1.4
- 1.4 Linux   1.5
  - 1.4.1 The Kernel   1.5
  - 1.4.2 Important Linux Commands   1.6
- 1.5 Translation Hierarchy   1.7
  - 1.5.1 Translation Hierarchy   1.8
- 1.6 Eclipse IDE   1.8
  - 1.6.1 Starting Eclipse   1.8
  - 1.6.2 Create Java Project   1.10
  - 1.6.3 Create Java Class   1.11
  - 1.6.4 Write Java Code   1.12
  - 1.6.5 Run Your Code   1.12
  - 1.6.6 Console Output   1.12
- 1.7 Programming Languages   1.13
  - 1.7.1 Types of Programming Languages   1.13
    - 1.7.1.1 Low Level Languages   1.13
    - 1.7.1.2 High Level Languages   1.14
  - 1.7.2 Characteristics of a Good Programming Language   1.16
- 1.8 Introduction to LISP : List Processing Language   1.18
- 1.9 MATLAB   1.18
- 1.10 Documentation   1.19
  - 1.10.1 Need for Documenting Programs and Software   1.20
  - 1.10.2 Forms of Documentation   1.20
- Multiple Choice Question   1.21

2. Introduction   2.1 – 2.40

2.1	Algorithm	2.1
2.2	Generalized Algorithm	2.2
	2.2.1 Advantages of Generalized Algorithms	2.2
2.3	Avoiding Infinite Loops in Algorithms	2.3
2.4	Methods of avoid Infinite Loops	2.3
	2.4.1 Controlling loops by Using a Counter	2.4
	2.4.2 By Using a Sentinel Value	2.5
2.5	Representing an Algorithms	2.5
	2.5.1 Representing an Algorithm as a Program	2.6
	2.5.2 Representing an Algorithm as a Flowchart	2.6
	2.5.3 Representing an Algorithm as a Pseudo Code	2.9
2.6	Program Planning	2.10
	2.6.1 Need of Program Planning or Designing	2.10
	2.6.2 Program Planning Tools	2.11
	2.6.3 Advantages of Program Planning Tools	2.14
2.7	Importance of use of Indentation of Programming	2.14
2.8	Structured Programming Concepts	2.15
	2.8.2 "Go to" statement	2.16
2.9	How all Programs can be written using Sequence Logic, Selection Logic and Iteration (or looping Logic)	2.17
	2.9.1 Sequence Logic	2.17
	2.9.1.1 Basic structure of sequence logic	2.18
	2.9.1.2 Generalized Flowchart for Sequence Logic	2.18
	2.9.1.3 Example of Sequence Logic	2.18
	2.9.2 Selection Logic	2.18
	2.9.2.1 Basic Structure of Selection Logic	2.19
	2.9.2.2 Example for Selection Logic	2.20
	2.9.3 Iteration (Repetition) Logic	2.20
	2.9.3.1 Basic Structure of Selection Logic	2.21
2.10	Functions	2.22
	2.10.1 Structure of a Function	2.22
	Multiple Choice Question	2.23

3. C Programming — 3.1 – 3.54

- 3.1 Introduction to Programming Languages — 3.1
- 3.2 Introduction to C Languages — 3.2
- 3.3 Character Set — 3.6
- 3.4 Constants — 3.7
- 3.5 Variables — 3.8
- 3.6 Keywords — 3.9
- 3.7 Operator and Operator Precedence — 3.10
- 3.8 Statements — 3.12
- 3.9 Input/Output (I/O) Operations — 3.13
- 3.10 Preprocessor Directives — 3.14
- 3.11 Pointers — 3.14
- 3.12 Arrays — 3.15
- 3.13 Strings — 3.16
- 3.14 User Define Data Types — 3.18
- Multiple Choice Question — 3.19

4. C Programming — 4.1 – 4.34

- 4.1 Introduction to Control Structure — 4.1
    - 4.1.1 Conditional Branching — 4.2
        - 4.1.1.1 Basic Structure of Selection Logic — 4.2
        - 4.1.1.2 Switch Statements — 4.4
    - 4.1.2 Unconditional Branching — 4.5
- 4.2 Loop Structure — 4.6
    - 4.2.1 Pretest loop Structure — 4.7
    - 4.2.2 Post Test Loop Structure — 4.8
- 4.3 Functions — 4.9
    - 4.3.1 Parameter Passing by Value — 4.11
    - 4.3.2 Parameter Passing by reference — 4.13
- 4.4 Main Functions — 4.14
    - 4.4.1 Main Function with argv, argc[] — 4.14
- 4.5 Testing and Debugging — 4.15
    - 4.5.1 Debugging — 4.15
    - 4.5.2 Testing — 4.15
- Multiple Choice Question — 4.16
- **Laboratory Assignments** — L.1 1.1-1.26

Unit 1
INTRODUCTION

Syllabus

Introduction to Open Source Operating Systems and Programming Languages, Introduction to Bharat Operating System (BOSS) GNU/Linux users model GUI, System Folders, study Commands (Using command terminal) with switches : ls, Directory Commands, Change user, privileges, passwords, tty, who, config, make, rpm, yum, sudo, Shutdown.

Eclipse Editor, Compiler, Linker, Libraries, GUI, Configuring Programming Environments: C, C++, Java, Python (Pydev), Output, Debug windows.

Introduction to types of Programming Languages – Machine-level, Assembly level and High-level Languages, Scripting Languages, Natural Languages; Their relative Advantages and Limitations. Characteristics of a Good Programming Language; Selecting a Language out of many available languages for coding an application;

1.1 Introduction to Operating System

1.1.1 Operating System

An operating system (OS) is a collection of software that manages computer hardware resources and provides common services for computer programs.

The operating system is a vital component of the system software in a computer system.

Application programs usually require an operating system to function.

For hardware functions such as input and output and memory allocation, the operating system acts as an intermediary between programs and the computer hardware.

1.1.2 Types of Operating System

1. Real-time

A real-time operating system is a multitasking operating system that aims at executing real-time applications. Real-time operating systems often use specialized scheduling algorithms so that they can achieve a deterministic nature of behavior. The main objective of real-time operating systems is their quick and predictable response to events. It has an event-driven or time-sharing design and often aspects of both.

2. Multi-user

A multi-user operating system allows multiple users to access a computer system at the same time. Time-sharing systems and internet servers can be classified as multi-user systems as they enable multiple-user access to a computer through the sharing of time. Single-user operating systems have only one user but may allow multiple programs to run at the same time.

3. Multi-tasking vs. single-tasking

A multi-tasking operating system allows more than one program to be running at a time. A single-tasking system has only one running program.

Multi-tasking can be of two types:

    (a) Pre-emptive and

    (b) Co-operative.

In **pre-emptive multitasking,** the operating system slices the CPU time and dedicates one slot to each of the programs. Unix-like operating systems such as **Solaris** and **Linux** support pre-emptive multitasking.

Cooperative multitasking is achieved by relying on each process to give time to the other processes in a defined manner. **16-bit versions of Microsoft Windows** used **cooperative** multi-tasking.

4. Distributed

A distributed operating system manages a group of independent computers and makes them appear to be a single computer. The development of networked computers that could be linked and communicate with each other gave rise to distributed computing. Distributed computations are carried out on more than one machine. When computers in a group work in cooperation, they make a distributed system.

5. Embedded

Embedded operating systems are designed to be used in **embedded computer systems.** They are designed to operate on small machines like PDAs. They are able to operate with a limited number of resources. They are very compact and extremely efficient by design. Windows **CE** and **Minix** 3 are some examples of embedded operating systems.

1.2 Open Source

Open source is a philosophy, or pragmatic methodology that promotes free redistribution and access to an end product's design and implementation details.

1.2.1 Open-Source Software (OSS)

It is computer software with its source code made available and licensed with an open-source license in which the copyright holder provides the rights to study, change and distribute the software for free to anyone and for any purpose.

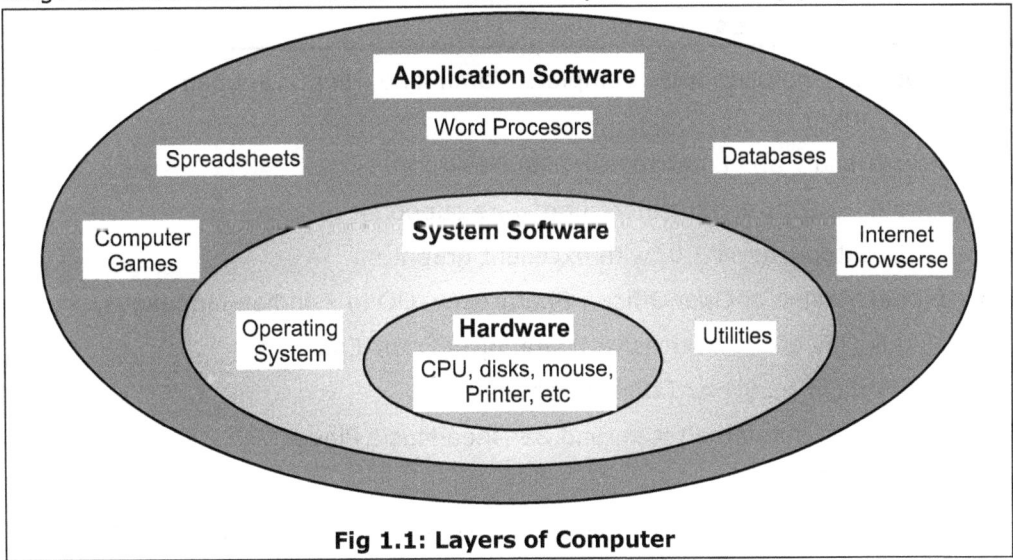

Fig 1.1: Layers of Computer

1.3 BOSS

Bharat Operating System Solutions (BOSS) is a free and open source computer operating system developed by the National Resource Centre for Free/Open Source Software (NRCFOSS) of India BOSS **GNU/Linux** is also known by the acronym BOSS.

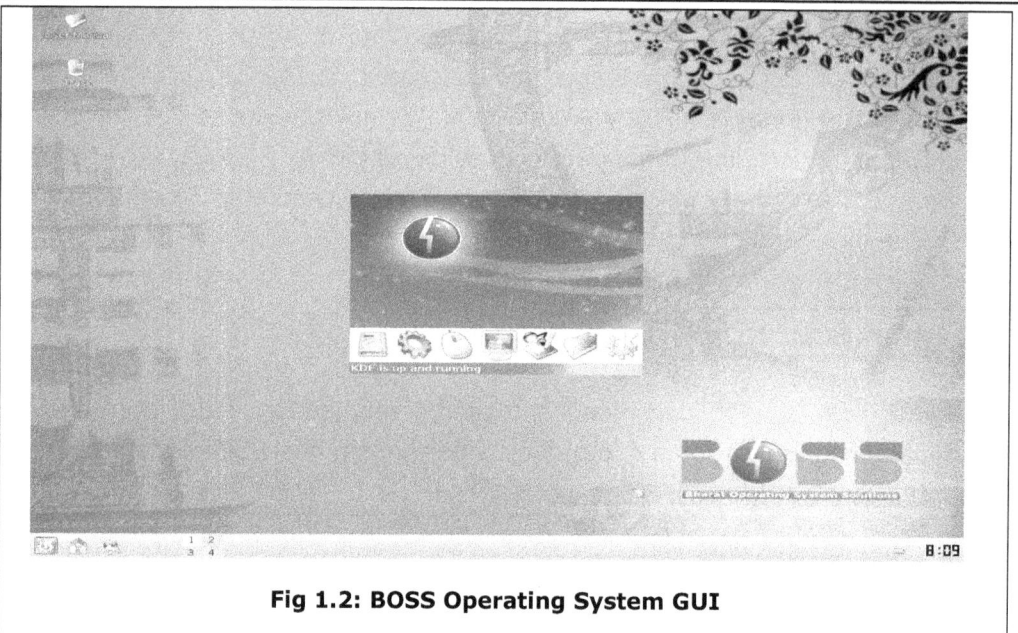

Fig 1.2: BOSS Operating System GUI

1.3.1 BOSS Features

- Graphical installer with Complete Tamil and Hindi Language support while installation.
- User friendly and Localized GNOME Desktop
- Kernel - 2.6.21.1-486 (more hardware support)
- 3D Desktop - beryl 2.0, with excellent graphics
- Indian version of OpenOffice, BharatheeyaOO in 7 Indian languages
- Plug & Play of the devices with Graphical Front-End
- Auto mount of all Hard Disk partitions
- Multimedia support - totem and Banshee Music Player
- Gnome – PPP
- Better usability of printers, scanners, webcam, digital camera, ,bluetooth, TV tuner card etc.
- Easy access to power management settings with GNOME Power Manager
- Migration Tool - Bulk Document converter
- BOSS Presentation tool – keyjnote
- Input Method - SCIM with Remington Keyboard Layout

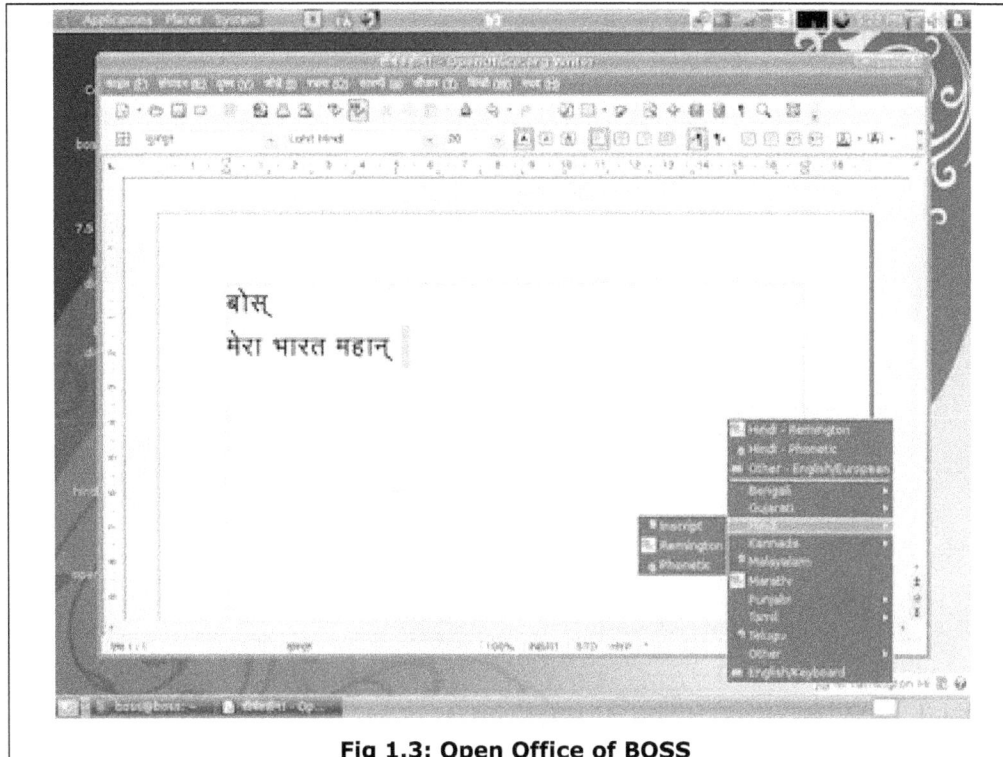

Fig 1.3: Open Office of BOSS

- BOSS GNU/Linux is available in the following eighteen languages of India, among the twenty-two constitutionally recognized languages of India:

Assamese	Bengali	Bodo	Gujarati	Hindi
Kannada	Kashmiri	Konkani	Maithili	Malayalam
Manipuri	Marathi	Oriya	Punjabi	Sanskrit
Tamil	Telugu	Urdu		

1.4 Linux

Linux is a **free, multi-threading, multiuser** operating system that has been ported to several different platforms and processor architectures.

1.4.1 The Kernel

The **kernel** is the heart of a Linux system. It controls the **resources, memory,** schedules processes and their access to CPU and is responsible of communication between software and hardware components. The kernel provides the lowest-level abstraction layer for the resources like memory, CPU and I/O devices. Applications that want to perform any function with these resources communicate with the kernel using system calls.

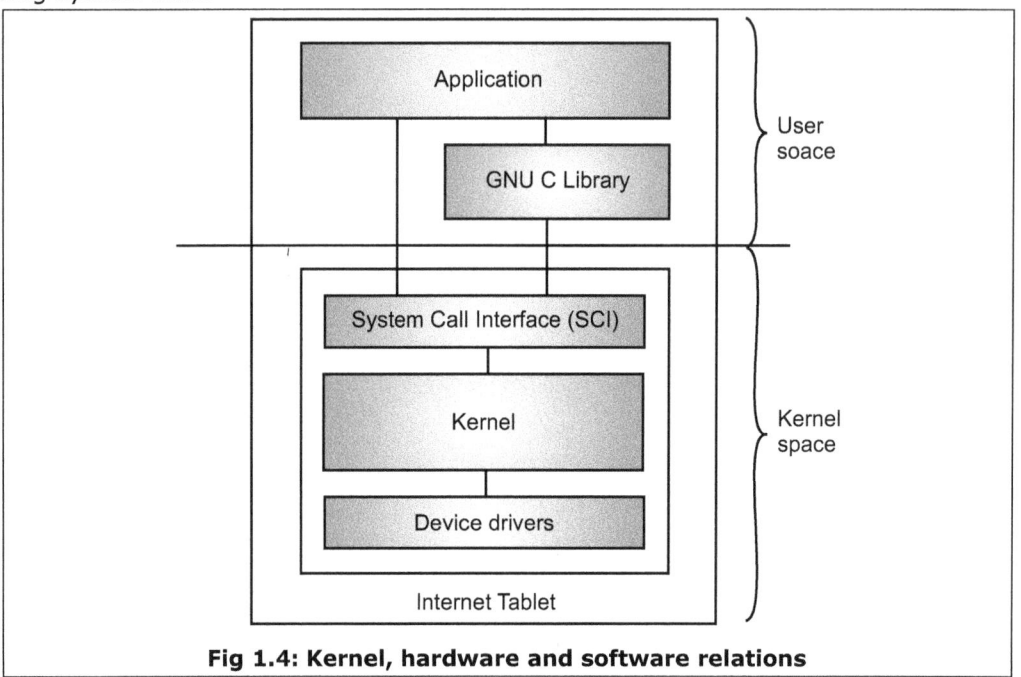

Fig 1.4: Kernel, hardware and software relations

1.4.2 Important Linux Commands

ls	List directory contents
man	This command brings up the online Unix manual.
pwd	Present working directory- Shows what directory (folder) you are in.
cd	Changes directories.
mkdir dirName	Creates a directory with name dirName
rmdir dirName	Removes a directory dirName.
vim	Vi Improved, a programmers text editor
find	Search for files in a directory hierarchy
history	Prints recently used commands

cal	Command to see calender for any specific month or a complete year
echo	Print message on the terminal
passwd	Allows you to change your password
mv	Change the name of a directory
cp	Copy files and directories
shutdown	Bring the system down
yum	It is an interactive, automated update program which can be used for maintaining systems using rpm
chmod	Change file access permissions

1.5 Translation Hierarchy

It describes the four steps in transforming a C program in a file on a disk into a program running on a computer.

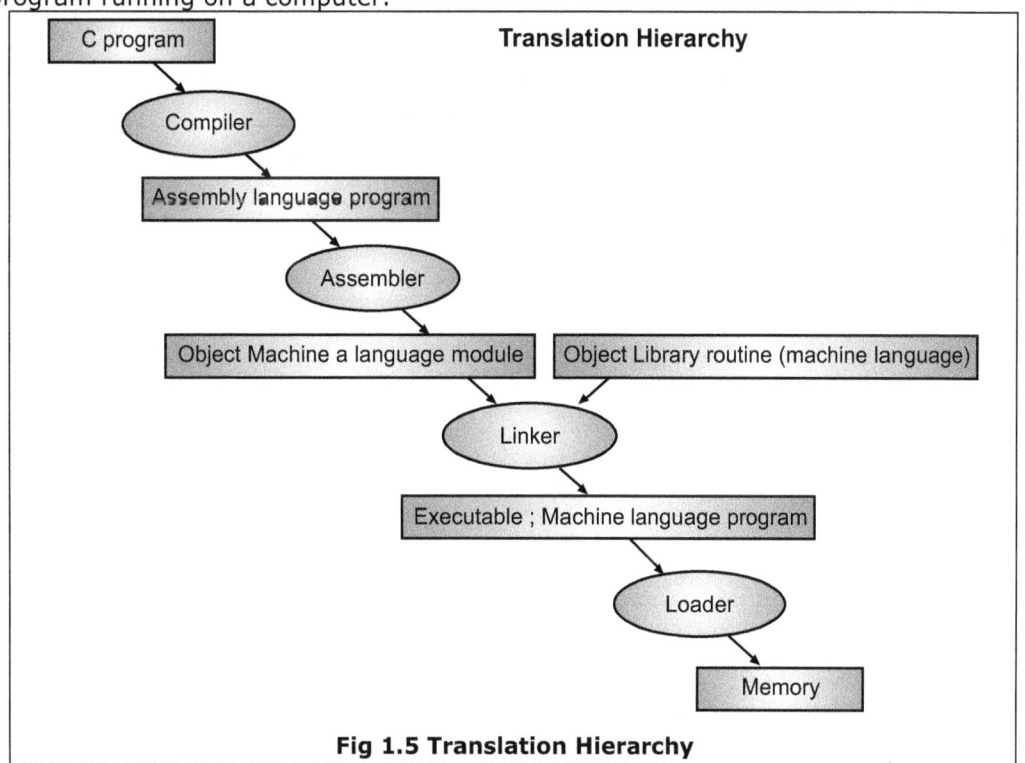

Fig 1.5 Translation Hierarchy

1.5.1 Translation Hierarchy

- **Compiler**–Translates high level language program into assembly language
- **Assembler**–Converts assembly language programs into object files. Object files contain a combination of machine instructions, data, and information needed to place instructions properly in memory.
- **Linker** - Tool that merges the object files produced by separate compilation or assembly and creates an executable file.
- **Loader-** Part of the OS that brings an executable file residing on disk into memory and starts it running

1.6 Eclipse IDE

- Eclipse is a multi-language Integrated Development Environment(IDE) comprising a base workspace and an extensible plug-in system for customizing the environment.
- It is written mostly in **Java.**
- It can be used to develop applications in Java and, by means of various plug-ins, other programming languages including Ada, C, C++, COBOL, Fortran, Haskell, JavaScript, Perl, PHP, Python, R, Ruby (including Ruby on Rails framework), Scala, Clojure, Groovy, Scheme, and Erlang.

1.6.1 Starting Eclipse

- To start Eclipse double-click on the **eclipse.exe .**

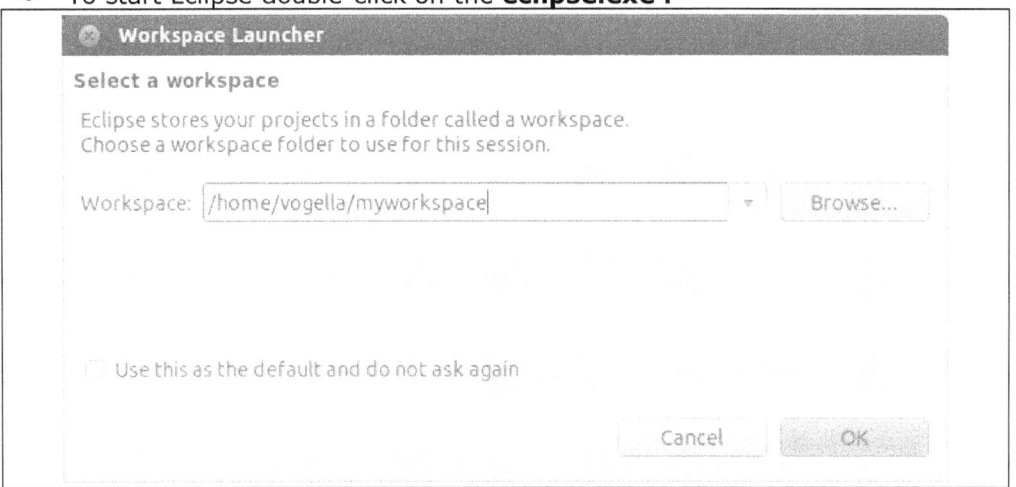

- The system will prompt you for a **workspace.** The *workspace* is the place in which you work.
- Select an empty directory and press the **OK** button.
- Eclipse starts and shows the Welcome page.

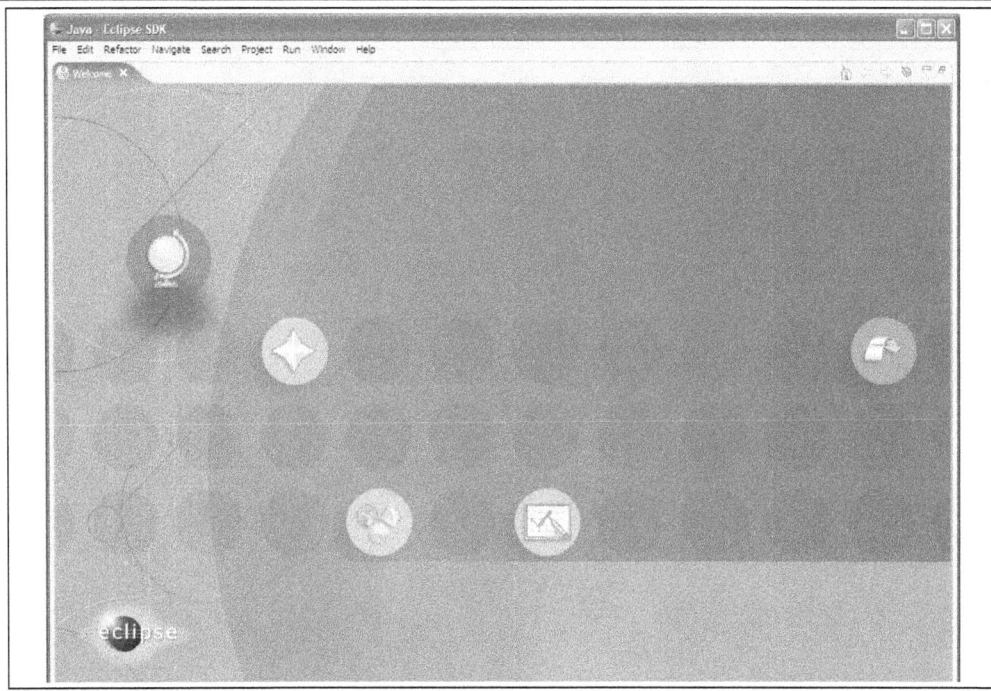

After closing the welcome screen you see a screen similar to the following screenshot.

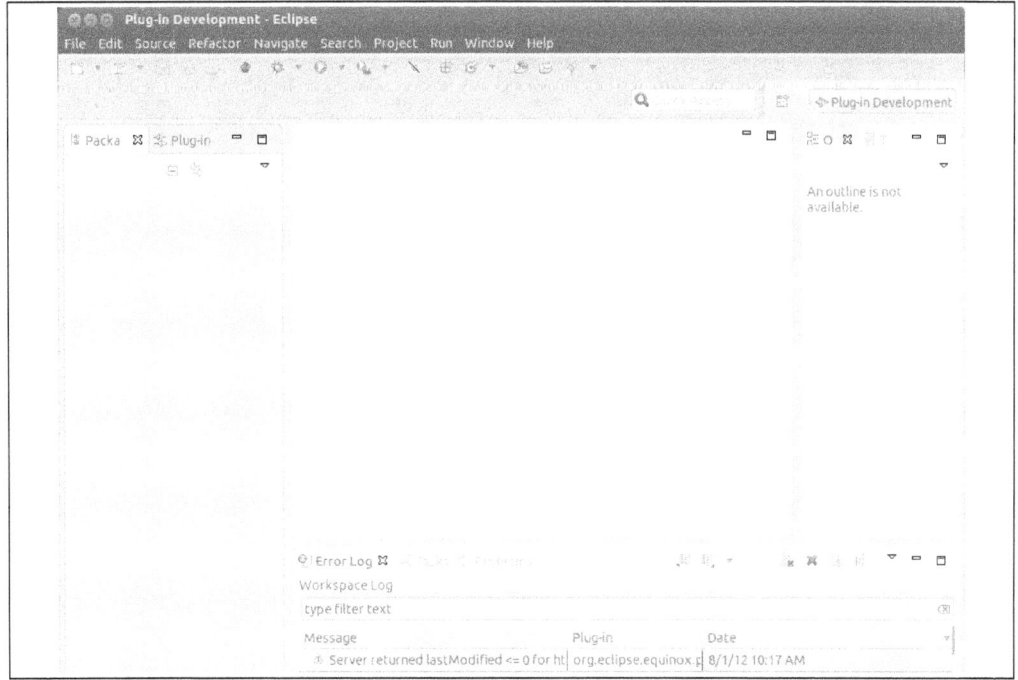

1.6.2 Create Java Project

Select from the menu File --> New --> Java Project.

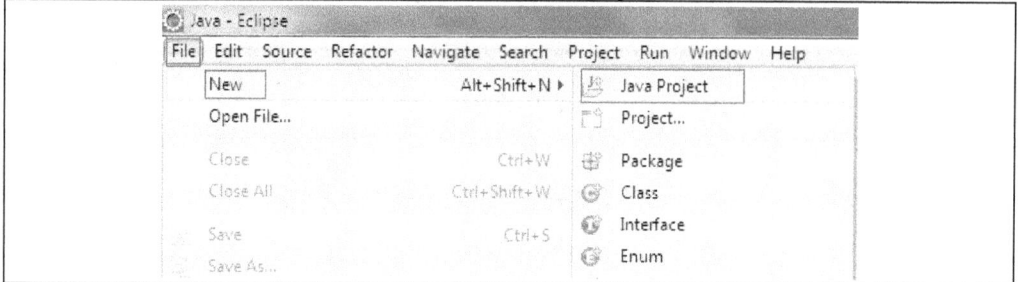

Enter "HelloWorld" as the project name. Keep rest of the settings as it is as shown in the following screenshot.

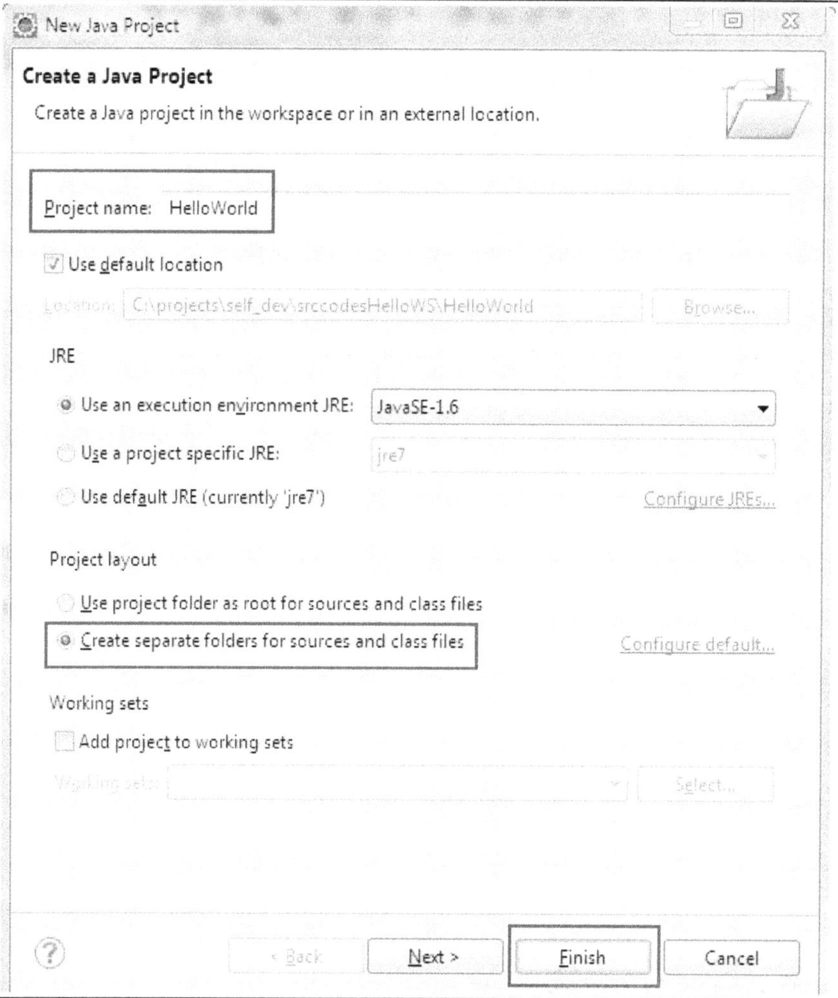

FPL – I ENGG. (F.E. SEM. I)   INTRODUCTION

Click "Finish" button and Eclipse IDE will generate the java project automatically.

1.6.3 Create Java Class

Right click on 'com.srccodes.example' package and select from context menu New --> Class.

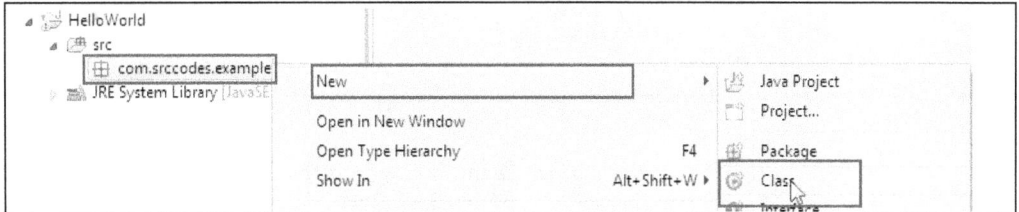

Write "HelloWorld" in the 'Name' field and select the check-box for 'public static void main(String[] args)'.

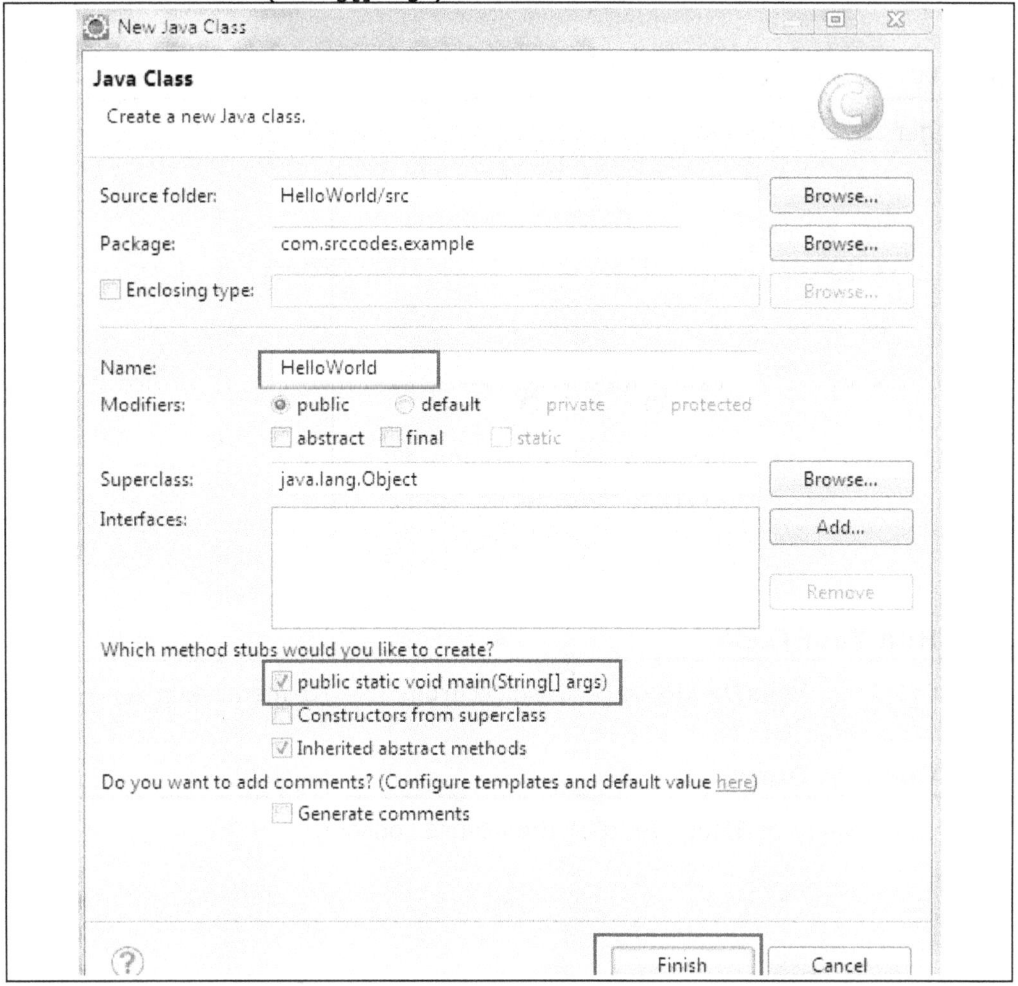

Click "Finish" button. Eclipse will generate a java class and open the same in the java editor as shown below.

```
HelloWorld.java
    package com.srccodes.example;

    public class HelloWorld {
        /**
         * @param args
         */
        public static void main(String[] args) {
            // TODO Auto-generated method stub

        }

    }
```

1.6.4 Write Java Code

Edit the generated 'HelloWord' java class as per the following code.

```java
package com.srccodes.example;

public class HelloWorld {
    /**
     * @param args
     */
    public static void main(String[] args) {
        System.out.println("Hello World");
    }
}
```

1.6.5 Run Your Code

Right click on 'HelloWorld java' and select from context menu 'Run As' --> 'Java Application'.

1.6.6 Console Output

Your code will print 'Hello World' in the eclipse console.

```
Problems  @ Javadoc  Declaration  Console
<terminated> HelloWorld [Java Application] C:\instld_soft\self_d(
Hello World
```

1.7 Programming Languages

A programming language is an artificial language designed to communicate instructions to a machine, particularly a computer. Programming languages can be used to create programs that control the behavior of a machine and/or to express algorithms precisely.

1.7.1 Types of Programming Languages

Basically, languages are divided into two categories according to their interpretation.

(i) Low Level Languages

(ii) High Level Languages

1.7.1.1 Low Level Languages

Low level computer languages are machine codes or close to it. Computer cannot understand instructions given in high level languages or in English. It can only understand and execute instructions given in the form of machine language i.e. language of 0 and 1. There are two types of low level languages:

1. Machine Language.
2. Assembly Language

1. Machine Language: It is the lowest and most elementary level of programming language and was the first type of programming language to be developed Machine Language is basically the only language which computer can understand In fact, a manufacturer designs a computer to obey just one language, its machine code, which is represented inside the computer by a string of binary digits (bits) 0 and 1. The symbol 0 stands for the absence of electric pulse and 1 for the presence of an electric pulse . Since a computer is capable of recognizing electric signals, therefore, it understand machine language.

Advantages of Machine Language

(i) It makes fast and efficient use of the computer.

(ii) It requires no translator to translate the code i.e.Directly understood by the computer.

Disadvantages of Machine Language

(i) All operation codes have to be remembered.

(ii) All memory addresses have to be remembered.

(iii) It is hard to amend or find errors in a program written in the machine language.

(iv) These languages are machine dependent

(v) Machine language can be used on only one type of computer

2. Assembly Language : It was developed to overcome some of the many inconveniences of machine language. This is another low level but a very important language in which operation codes and operands are given in the form of alphanumeric symbols instead of 0's and 1's. These alphanumeric symbols will be known as mnemonic codes and can have maximum up to 5 letter combination e.g. ADD for addition, SUB for subtraction, START, LABEL etc Because of this feature it is also known as **'Symbolic Programming Language'.** This language is also very difficult and needs a lot of practice to master it because very small.

English support is given to this language. The language mainly helps in compiler orientations. The instructions of the assembly language will also be converted to machine codes by language translator to be executed by the computer.

Advantages of Assembly Language

(i) It is easier to understand and use as compared to machine language.

(ii) It is easy to locate and correct errors.

(iii) It is modified easily.

Disadvantages of Assembly Language

(i) Like machine language it is also machine dependent.

(ii) Since it is machine dependent therefore programmer should have the knowledge of the hardware also.

1.7.1.2 High Level Languages

High level computer languages give formats close to English language and the purpose of developing high level languages is to enable people to write programs easily and in their own native language environment (English). High-level languages are basically symbolic languages that use English words and/or mathematical symbols rather than mnemonic codes. Each instruction in the high level language is translated into many machine language instructions thus showing one-to-many translation

Types of High Level Languages

Many languages have been developed for achieving different variety of tasks, some are fairly specialized others are quite general purpose.

These are categorized according to their use as follows:

(a) Algebraic Formula : Type Processing. These languages are oriented towards the computational procedures for solving mathematical and statistical problem

Examples :
- **BASIC** (Beginners All Purpose Symbolic Instruction Code).
- **FORTRAN** (Formula Translation).
- **PL/I** (Programming Language, Version 1).
- **ALGOL** (Algorithmic Language).
- **APL** (A Programming Language).

(b) Business Data Processing:
- These languages emphasize their capabilities for maintaining data processing procedures and files handling problems.

Examples :
- COBOL (Common Business Oriented Language).
- RPG (Report Program Generator)

(c) String and List Processing : These are used for string manipulation including search for patterns, inserting and deleting characters.

Examples :
- LISP (List Processing).
- Prolog (Program in Logic).

(d) Object Oriented Programming Language

In OOP, the computer program is divided into objects.

Examples :
- C++
- Java

(e) Visual programming language : these are designed for building Windows-based applications

Examples :
- Visual Basic
- Visual Java
- Visual C

Advantages of High Level Language

Following are the advantages of a high level language:

(i) User-friendly.

(ii) Similar to English with vocabulary of words and symbols

(iii) It is easier to learn.

(iv) They require less time to write.

(v) They are easier to maintain.

(vi) Problem oriented rather than 'machine' based.

(vii) Program written in a high-level language can be translated into many machine language and therefore can run on any computer for which there exists an appropriate translator.

(viii) It is independent of the machine on which it is used i.e. Programs developed in high level language can be run on any computer.

Disadvantages of High Level Language

(i) A high-level language has to be translated into the machine language by a translator.

(ii) The object code generated by a translator might be inefficient compared to an equivalent assembly language program.

1.7.2 Characteristics of a Good Programming Language

Several characteristics believed to be important with respect to making a programming language good are briefly discussed below.

1. Simplicity

A good programming language must be simple and easy to learn and use. For example, BASIC is liked by many programmers only because of its simplicity. Thus, a good programming language should provide a programmer with a clear, simple and unified set of concepts which can be easily grasped It is also easy to develop and implement a compiler or an interpreter for a programming language that is simple. However, the power needed for the language should not be sacrificed for simplicity. The overall simplicity of a programming language strongly affects the readability of the programs written in that language, and programs that are easier to read and understand are also easier to maintain.

2. Naturalness

A good language should be natural for the application area it has been designed That is, it should provide appropriate operators, data structures, control structures, and a natural syntax in order to facilitate the users to code their problem easily and efficiently. FORTRAN and COBOL are good examples of scientific and business languages respectively that posses high degree of naturalness.

3. Abstraction

Abstraction means the ability to define and then use complicated structures or operations in ways that allow many of the details to be ignored The degree of abstraction allowed by a programming language directly affects its writability. For example, object-oriented languages support high degree of abstraction. Hence writing programs in object-oriented languages is much easier. Object-oriented languages also support reusability of program segments due to its feature.

4. Efficiency

The program written in good programming language are efficiently translated into machine code, are efficiently executed, and acquires as little space in the memory as possible. That is, a good programming language is supported with a good language translator (a compiler or an interpreter) that gives due consideration to space and time efficiency.

5. Structured

Structured means that the language should have necessary features to allow its users to write their programs based on the concepts of structured programming. This property of a language greatly affects the ease with which a program may be written, tested, and maintained Moreover, it forces a programmer to look at a problem in a logical way so that fewer errors are created while writing a program for the problem.

6. Compactness

In a good programming language, programmers should be able to express intended operation concisely. A verbose language can tax the programmer's sheer writing stamina and thus reduce its usefulness. COBOL is generally not liked by many programmers because it is verbose in nature and compactness.

7. Locality

A good programming language should be such that while writing a program, a programmer need not jump around visually as the text of the program is prepared This allows the programmer to concentrate almost solely on the part of the program around the statements currently being worked with. COBOL lacks locality because data definitions are separated from processing statements, perhaps by many pages of code.

8. Extensibility

A good programming language should allow extension through simple, natural, and elegant mechanisms. Almost all languages provide subprogram definition mechanisms for this purpose, but there are some languages that are rather weak in this aspect.

9. Suitability to its Environment

Depending upon the type of application for which a programming language has been designed, the language must also be made suitable to its environment. For example, a language designed for real time applications must be interactive in nature. On the other hand, languages used for data processing jobs like pay-roll, stores accounting, etc, may be designed to be operative in batch mode.

1.8 Introduction to LISP : List Processing Language

- LISP is the premier language for Artificial Intelligence applications.
- Special focus on symbolic processing and symbol.
- It is a dynamic language: editing changes take effect immediately, without the need for recompilation.
- It is primarily a functional language: all work can be done via function composition and recursion.
- There is no "main program" the programmer can call any function from the input prompt.
- Provides built-in support for lists ("everything is a list").
- Automatic storage management (no need to keep track of memory allocation).
- Interactive environment, which allows programs to be developed step by step. That is, if a change is to be introduced, only changed functions need to be recompiled.

1.9 MATLAB

- MATLAB (matrix laboratory) is a numerical computing environment and fourth-generation programming language.
- Developed by MathWorks.
- MATLAB allows matrix manipulations, plotting of functions and data, implementation of algorithms, creation of user interfaces, and interfacing with programs written in other languages, including C, C++, Java, and Fortran.

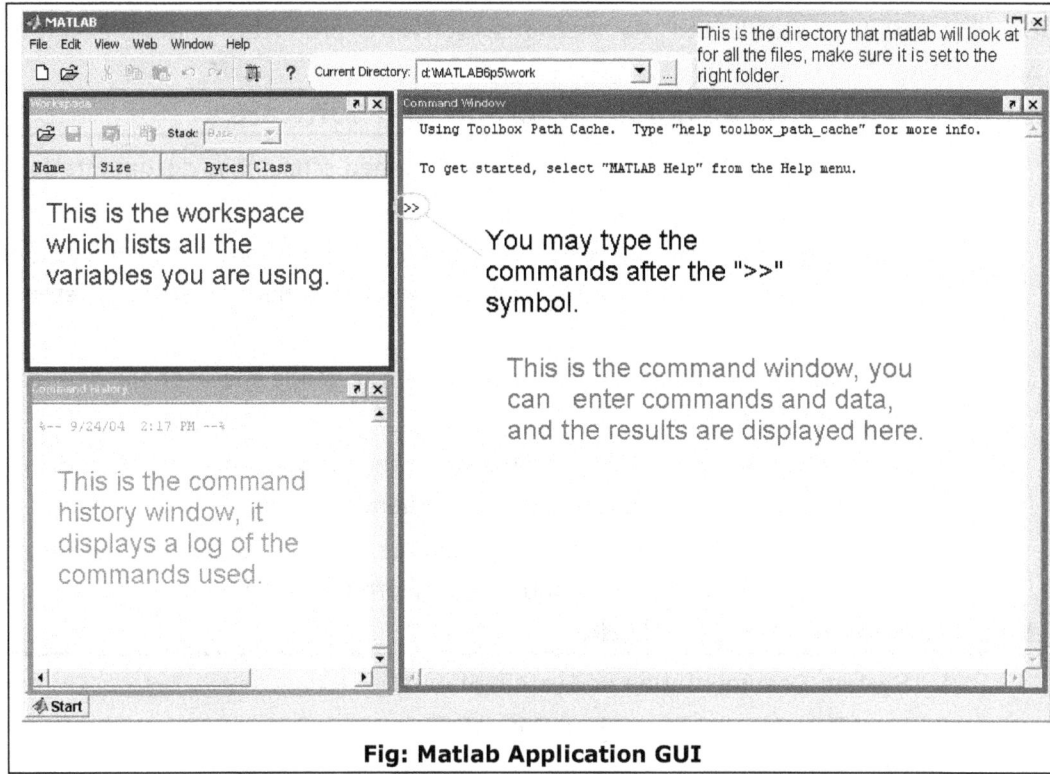

Fig: Matlab Application GUI

GNU Octave

- GNU Octave is a high-level programming language, primarily intended for numerical computations.
- This is open-source free license software.
- All command which work in MATLAB can be used in this software.
- Available under GNU's General Public License.
- It is particularly designed for matrix computations like solving simultaneous equations, computing eigenvectors and eigenvalues.

1.10 Documentation

Software documentation or source code documentation is written text that accompanies computer software. It either explains how it operates or how to use it, and may mean different things to people in different roles.

Common types of documentation include user guides, white papers, on-line help, quick-reference guides. It is less common to see hard-copy (paper) documentation.

Documentation is distributed via websites, software products, and other on-line applications.

1.10.1 Need for Documenting Programs and Software

- For software to be used properly and maintained efficiently, documentation is needed.
- To run the software system properly, the users need documentation, traditionally called a ***user guide,*** that shows how to use the software step by step.
- User guides usually contains a tutorial section to guide the user through each feature of the software.
- When developing software, documentation and design and is first and most critical component in any software development lifecycle.
- The design documentation is the single source of truth for developers and the business to clearly outline how and why any proposed development is viable.

1.10.2 Forms of Documentation

1. System Documentation or System Manual
2. User Documentation or User Manual
3. Comments

1. System Documentation or System Manual

System documentation defines the software itself. It should be written so that the software can be maintained and modified by people other than the original developers.

2. User Documentation or User Manual

The User Manual contains all essential information for the user to make full use of the information system. This manual includes a description of the system functions and capabilities, contingencies and alternate modes of operation, and step-by-step procedures for system access and use.

For a formal release of a software application following five areas should be documented:

1. Functional Description of Software
2. Installation Instructions
3. Introductory Manual
4. Reference Manual
5. System Administrator's Guide

3. Comments
- It is form of internal documentation.
- Used to understand logic of program.
- Do not contain any programming instruction , so it is ignored by language translator.
- Single line comment: //.
- Block of comment: /*   */.

Multiple Choice Questions

1. A translator program that translates an assembly code into machine code is known as _____
   - A) Compiler
   - B) Assembler
   - C) Interpreter
   - D) Loader.

2. Which of the following statements are related to the machine language?
   - A) Difficult to learn
   - B) First-generation language
   - C) Machine-dependent
   - D) All of the above.

3. FORTRAN is a _____
   - A) General Purpose and Procedural Language
   - B) Imperative programming language
   - C) Both a and b
   - D) None of above.

4. An assembly language consist of _____ instructions.
   - A) Mnemonics
   - B) Opcodes
   - C) Operands
   - D) Fields.

5. Which of the following language does not allow a programmer to substitute name or symbol for numbers?
   - A) Assembly level
   - B) Machine level
   - C) High level
   - D) 4GL.

6. The software tool that is used for linking modules together is called_____.
   - A) Editor
   - B) Linker
   - C) Compiler
   - D) Debugger.

7. A component of a computer that locates a given program or application from the offline storage, loads it into the main memory and facilitates its execution is called _____.
   A) Interpreter
   B) Compiler
   C) Linker
   D) Loader.

8. 'C' is a _____ .
   A) High level language
   B) Low level language
   C) Machine language
   D) Binary language.

9. _____ is a case sensitive language.
   A) C++
   B) PASCAL
   C) BASIC
   D) None of the above.

10. Operating system is used to
    A) Switch the processor between processes
    B) Decide the way parameters must be passed from one function to another
    C) Allocate memory to program variables during execution
    D) Optimize code generated by a compiler.

11. Which of the following is not related to machine language?
    A) opcode
    B) data movement operations
    C) instruction set
    D) none of these.

12. Which of the following is not case sensitive language?
    A) C
    B) JAVA
    C) C++
    D) none of these.

13. RPG is acronym used for
    A) Remote Program Generator
    B) Recursive Program Generator
    C) Report Program Generator
    D) Recurrent Program Generator.

14. In which of the following language the opcodes are used
    A) assembly language
    B) machine language
    C) high-level language
    D) none of these.

15. In which of the following language a program can be written using symbolic names?
    A) assembly language
    B) high-level language
    C) machine language
    D) all the above.

16. The structured programming languages are also known as _____ languages.
    A) Object oriented   B) Procedure oriented
    C) Modular programming   D) All the above.
17. The Language made of streams of 0's & 1's is called as a _____.
    A) Symbolic language   B) High level Language
    C) machine Language   D) Algorithm.
18. Each line of _____ program consists of four columns known as fields
    A) Machine language   B) Assembly language
    C) Scripting Language   D) Pascal.
19. Which of the following is a high-level language?
    A) BASIC   B) PASCAL
    C) FORTRAN   D) All of the above.
20. PASCAL is a
    A) Low level language   B) Machine level language
    C) High Level language   D) Object oriented language.
21. What is the correct file extention for a C++ program?
    A) C++   B) C   C) CPP   D) CCP.
22. Fortran is
    A) General purpose   B) Procedural
    C) Imperative programming D) All of above.
23. Line editor and _____ are the types of editor.
    A) Function editor   B) Module editor
    C) Screen editor   D) None of these.
24. _____ loads a given program from a disk.
    A) Linker   B) Compiler
    C) Interpreter   D) Loader.
25. _____ translates whole program written in high language to a machine language.
    A) Compiler   B) Interpreter
    C) Linker   D) Loader.
26. The language that the computer can understand and execute is called
    A) Low-level machine language. B) High-level language.
    C) Assembly Language.   D) None of the above.

27. Which of the following factors should be considered while selecting a programming language for application development?
    A) Nature of application   B) Ease of learning the language
    C) Familarity with the language   D) All of the above.

28. Interpreter is used to convert
    A) Low level to Machine level   B) High level to Machine level
    C) Assembly to low level   D) None of these.

29. Which of the following languages is effective for mathematical calculations
    A) Fortran.   B) C
    C) PASCAL   D) All of the above.

30. _____ governs the sequencing of control through program.
    A) Control structure   B) Control program
    C) Control time   D) All of the above.

31. Instructions are encoded as number is a feature of _____ .
    A) Assembly language   B) High level language
    C) Machine language   D) C language.

32. A complier reads the entire program & converts it in to a_____ .
    A) Machine code   B) C code
    C) C++ code   D) High level.

33. Which of the following statement is/are correct?
    A) Linker is a program that takes one or more object files generated by a compiler and assembles them into a single executable program.
    B) Linker is a program that takes one or more source program files and assembles them into a single executable program.
    C) Linker is a program that translates a high-level language program into its equivalent object code.
    D) None of the above.

34. Which of the Following is not a Translator program?
    A) Assembler   B) Compiler   C) Interpreter   D) Linker.

35. A Linker
    A) combines different modules of the programme.
    B) allows user to write a programme.
    C) finds out errors.
    D) is used to debug a programme.

36. 'C' can be used on _____ platforms.
    A) MS-DOS operating system.   B) Linux operating system.
    C) Windows operating system. D) All the above.
37. Which of the following is an assembly language instruction?.00E+1ADD AX, 1X = X + Y. SET! X Y).B Consider the following statements:
    i) Compilers and Interpreters are used to find errors
    ii) Compilers are faster when compared to the interpreters Which of the following statement is correct?
    A) Both the statements are correct.
    B) Only first statement is correct.
    C) Only Second statement is correct.
    D) Both the statements are wrong.
38. Which of the following language is easy to debug ?
    A) assembly language.   B) machine language.
    C) all high-level languages.   D) all the above.
39. Which of the following saves the generated object code ?
    A) Interpreter.   B) Linker.
    C) Compiler.   D) Loader.
40. Advantages of interpreters over compliers are _____.
    A) they are less complex programs than compliers
    B) they need less memory space for execution than compliers
    C) syntax error in a program statement is detected during processing of that statement
    D) all of them.
41. A source program is
    A) a program written in a machine language.
    B) a program to be translated into machine language.
    C) a machine language translation of a program.
    D) None of these.
42. FORTRAN stands for-
    A) Foreign translater.   B) Formula Transmission.
    C) Formula Translator.   D) Formula Transaction.
43. Which one of the following is an example of machine language?
    A) ADD r1,r2   B) 10010111
    C) y-y+2   D) printf ("Welcome");.

Unit 1 | 1.25

44. Assembly languages are High Level languages
    A) The statement is correct.
    B) The statement is wrong.
    C) The statement is partially correct.
    D) None of above.
45. Which files are linked by a Linker?
    A) Source Files   B) Object Files
    C) Executable Files   D) Text Files.
46. Which of the following is a business oriented language?
    A) FORTRAN   B) PASCAL   C) C   D) COBOL.
47. Which of the following is a low level language?
    A) C   B) LISP
    C) Machin Level Lanaguage D) JAVA)
48. Which of the following language is best suited for system-level programming?
    A) BASIC   B) C   C) LISP   D) JAVA)
49. Which of the following sequence is correct?
    A) source code - compiler - object code - linker - executable code
    B) source code - linker - object code - compiler - executable code
    C) object code - compiler - source code - linker - executable code
    D) object code - linker - source code - compiler - executable code.
50. The computer software has been classified into two categories. They are _____.
    A) Hardware & Software
    B) Input & Output
    C) System Software & Application software
    D) Linker & Loader.
51. A 'C' program is portable means it _____.
    A) Can run on any machine
    B) can write on any machine
    C) can read from as well as write to any machine
    D) All of the above.
52. Which programming language is machine independent?
    A) Machine level language   B) Assembly level language
    C) High level language   D) Both A and B)

53. A program that aids in effective execution of user programs is called
    A) Application program
    B) System program
    C) Both System and Application program
    D) Neither System nor Application program.

54. _____ instruct the assembler to perform certain actions during the assembly of programs
    A) Assembler directives
    B) Compiler directives
    C) Declarative statements
    D) Imperative statements.

55. _____ is an example of a High Level language.
    A) C ++.
    B) Assembly language.
    C) JavA
    D) Both A and

56. Low level languages are _____ .
    A) Machine level language
    B) Assembly level language
    C) High level language
    D) Both A and B)

57. _____ language is understood by a computer without using translation. as ------
    A) assembly language
    B) symbolic language
    C) machine language
    D) higher level language.

58. Application software can be for
    A) Operating system
    B) Translator
    C) General-purpose application & Application specific solutions
    D) All of the above.

59. Which of the following is the easiest language to learn and use to write programs?
    A) high level language
    B) machine level language
    C) assembly level language
    D) middle level language.

60. Which of the following language is predecessor to C Programming Language?
    A) A
    B) B
    C) C++
    D) BCPL.

61. All computer languages can be broadly classified into following categories except
    A) High level language
    B) Middle level language
    C) Assembly language
    D) Machine level language.

Unit 1 | 1.27

62. What is the name of the latest Server Operating System developed by Microsoft?
    A) Windows NT
    B) Windows 2000
    C) Windows XP
    D) Windows 2003.

63. What is the name of the software that allows us to view web pages ?
    A) Browser
    B) Mail Client
    C) FTP Client
    D) Messenger.

64. Macromedia is a name of a company related with development of _____ products.
    A) Hardware
    B) Software
    C) Periperals
    D) Services.

65. The only language understood by any computer is :
    A) Machine Language
    B) Binary Language
    C) C
    D) Assembly Language.

66. Limitations of assembly language is/are
    A) It is machine dependent
    B) Machine level coding is required
    C) None
    D) Both A and B

67. Limitations of Assembly Language _____.
    A) It is machins dependent
    B) Machine level coding is required
    C) None
    D) A and B

68. Java Compiler produces
    A) Byte code
    B) Object Code
    C) Binary Code
    D) Hash Code.

69. Java Language is
    A) Low level language
    B) Machine level language
    C) Procedure Oriented language
    D) Object oriented language.

70. The long form of the word \"GUI\" is _____ .
    A) General User Interface
    B) Group Users of Internet
    C) Graphical User Interface
    D) Get Use and Iterate.

71. This is a multi-platform language that is especially useful in networking
    A) FORTRAN
    B) PERL
    C) JAVA
    D) ADA

72. Which of the following is not a procedural language?
    A) C
    B) PASCAL
    C) FORTRAN
    D) LISP.

73. Low level language uses _____
    A) English words   B) Mnemonic Codes
    C) Limited Grammer   D) Mathematical Symbols.

74. Which of the following Language is most suited for a procedure oriented program?
    A) C   B) Assembly
    C) Machine   D) None of the above.

75. A COBOL program is saved with a _____ file extension
    A) .cab   B) .cbl   C) .cpp   D) .coB)

76. C++ is a _____.
    A) Procedural Language   B) Object Oriented Language
    C) Assembly Language   D) None of above.

77. A Compiler is the _____.
    A) name given to computer operator
    B) part of digital machine to store information
    C) translator for translating a source code into the object code
    D) part of arithmatic logic unit.

78. Which of the following programming language is used for solving scientific & engineering problems?
    A) COBOL   B) C   C) SNOBOL   D) LISP.

79. All computers execute _____
    A) BASIC program   B) COBOL program
    C) Machine Language program   D) FORTRAN program.

80. Who invernted C++?
    A) Dennis Ritchie   B) Stroustrup
    C) Charles Babbage   D) John Macarty.

81. Which of the following language is Object Oriented Laguage?
    A) C   B) C++   C) LISP   D) COBOL.

82. CPU can execute _____ instructions
    A) ASSEMBLY level   B) Machine level
    C) C SOURCE level   D) INTERMIDIATE.

83. Which of the following translate and execute the given program statement-by-statement?
    A) compiler   B) assembler   C) interpreater D) linker.

84. Mnemonics are used in _____
    A) Assembly language program   B) C++ program
    C) Java program   D) C# program.

85. _____ programming deals with solving problems by identifiying the real world objects of the problem and the processing requirement of those objects and creating their simulations, processes and communications.
    A) Procedure Oriented   B) Object Oriented
    C) Functional programming   D) Logic programming.

86. _____ programs are composed of blocks, in which each block of statements starts with Begin and ends with End statements.
    A) BASIC   B) C   C) PASCAL   D) FORTRAN.

87. _____ is designed for Bussiness Data Proccessing applications.
    A) BASIC   B) COBOL   C) FORTRAN   D) C language.

88. Which of the following is not a High Level language?
    A) C   B) Assembly   C) C++   D) FORTRAN.

89. Capability to concurrently work on more than one task is called _____ .
    A) multipaging   B) multitasking
    C) demand paging   D) none of above.

90. Consider the following statements:
    a) Programming languages, like spoken languages, are means of communicating ideas
    b) Programming languages are intermediate between machine and programmer
    c) Language translators translate programs into machine
    A) Only B is true   B) Only B and C are true
    C) All are true   D) None is true.

91. Which of the following is an object oriented language?
    A) FORTRAN   B) COBOL   C) C++   D) PASCAL.

92. While translating a program _____ .
    A) An interpreter translates each statement only once, but a compiler translates each statement every time that statement is executed
    B) A compiler translates each statement only once, but a interpreter translates each statement every time that statement is executed
    C) Both compiler and interpreter translate each statement only once
    D) Both compiler and interpreter translate each statement every time that statement is executed

93. A source program is _____
    A) a program written in a machine language
    B) a program to be translated into machine language
    C) a machine language translation of a program
    D) None of these.

94. The operating system provides a service for _____.
    A) Language Translation
    B) File and Database Access
    C) Language Interpretation
    D) None of the above.

95. Java is a _____.
    A) Low-level language
    B) High level language
    C) Middle level language
    D) Machine language.

96. Which of the following is an application software?
    A) Tally
    B) Autocad
    C) MS-Office
    D) all of the above.

97. 'C' is _____ language
    A) Procedural
    B) Assembly
    C) Macne
    D) Object-orienteD

98. Which of the following language is/are difficult to modify?
    A) Machine-level
    B) Assembly-level
    C) Low-level
    D) High-level.

99. The Language that uses symbols and mnemonics to represent the various machine language instructions is called as _____.
    A) Spoken Language
    B) Machine-level Language
    C) Assembly Language
    D) Pseudocode.

100. A software utility that helps us to write, change and save programs is known as a _____.
    A) Editor
    B) Loader
    C) Linker
    D) Compiler.

101. Reading the program from the disk into memory is the function of _____.
    A) Interpreter
    B) Loader
    C) Editor
    D) Tester.

102. A program is written in a high level language. Which of the following system program is/are required to generate instructions understood by the computer and execute it?
    A) Linker
    B) Compiler and Assembler
    C) Loader
    D) All of the above.

103. The computer language that most closely resembles machine language is?
    A) Assembly Language
    B) COBOL
    C) FORTRAN
    D) High-level.

104. LISP stands for_____
    A) List Program.
    B) List Processing.
    C) List Processor.
    D) List Project.

105. Which of the following is an open source operating system?
    A) DOS
    B) WINDOWS
    C) LINUX
    D) DOS, WINDOWS and LINUX.

106. COBOL is a _____ .
    A) Common business oriented language
    B) Unstructured language
    C) Structured language
    D) Object-oriented language.

107. Types of programming languages are _____ .
    A) machine language, assembly language, high level language
    B) machine language, natural language, assembly language
    C) machine language, natural language, English
    D) All of the above.

108. Which among the following is a non-structured programming language ?
    A) Pascal
    B) C language
    C) FORTRAN
    D) All of the above.

109. GUI is an acronym for _____.
    A) General urgent interface
    B) Grand utility interface
    C) Graphical user interface
    D) Gaphic Utility Interface.

FPL – I ENGG. (F.E. SEM. I)   INTRODUCTION

110. The tool used by a programmer to convert a source program into a machine language e is called a _____ .
   A) compiler   B) linker
   C) language translator   D) text editor.

111. The _____ contains the programmer's original program code.
   A) Destination file   B) Executable file
   C) Object file   D) Source file.

112. Syntax error will be detected by_____.
   A) Loader   B) Linker
   C) Editor   D) Compiler.

113. PL/I stand for_____.
   A) programming language one   B) processing language one
   C) promting language one   D) none of these.

114. Which of the following is not an application software?
   A) Mouse driver   B) Microsoft OfficeC
   C) Oracle   D) Notepa

115. Computer software includes
   A) Application programs
   B) System programs
   C) Only Application programs
   D) Both Application and System Programs.

116. Assembly Language program is translated into machine code using _____
   A) Interpreter   B) Linker
   C) Editor   D) Assembler.

117. A_____ is also called as subprogram, subroutine, procedure
   A) Functions   B) Loops
   C) Control Structure   D) Variables.

118. Linkers are used_____
   A) To link library header files with programs
   B) To find syntax errors in the program
   C) To convert the source program to object code
   D) All of these.

Unit 1 | 1.33

119. C programs are converted into machine language with the help of
    A) An Editor   B) A Compiler
    C) An Operating System   D) An interpreter.

120. A Compiler is _____
    A) A combination of computer hardware and software
    B) A program which translates program written in a high-level language to some other high-level language
    C) A program which translates program written in a high-level language to a machine level language
    D) None of these.

121. The ____ is system software used to translate source program into object program.
    A) editor   B) Compiler   C) Linker   D) Interpreter.

122. Who invented the C Language?
    A) Dennis Ritchie
    B) Brian Kernighan and Dennis Ritchie
    C) Newton
    D) Enstin.

123. A_____ is a program written in such way that it can be brought into use by other programs.
    A) Main program   B) Subprogram
    C) GUI   D) None of the above.

124. which command is used to save a word file
    A) ctrl+s   B) alt+s
    C) shift+s   D) none of above.

125. Which of the following is/are System Software?
    A) MS WORD   B) MS WINDOWS
    C) MS EXCEL   D) MS ACCESS.

126. Operating system is_____.
    A) A collection of hardware components
    B) A collection of programs to manage system resources
    C) A collection of input-output devices
    D) None of the above.

127. Computer Software _____
    A) enhances the capabilities of the hardware machine
    B) increases the speed of central processing unit
    C) Both of the above
    D) Nome of the above.

128. Which of the following is not a computer language
    A) Assembly language   B) Binary language
    C) High Level language   D) Natural language.

129. The tool used by a programmer to convert source program to machine language code is called _____
    A) Compiler   B) Language translator
    C) Linker   D) Preprocessor.

130. Operating system_____.
    A) Manages system resources
    B) Provides a layered, user-friendly interface.
    C) Enables a programmer to draw a flowchart
    D) A and B

131. The software used to create programs is called _____
    A) Assembler   B) Compiler
    C) Editor   D) Linker.

132. Which of the following is not an operating system?
    A) Linux   B) Java Virtual Machine
    C) Windows   D) UNIX.

133. The process of improving programmer efficiency & changing his/her focus from the computer details, to the problem being solved led to the development of a _____.
    A) High level language   B) Symbolic Language
    C) Machine Language   D) none of the above.

134. Which of the following is an example of an application software?
    A) Language translator   B) Operating system
    C) Database management system D) Editor.

135. An Object module is linked to the standard functions necessary for running the program. This task is carried out by a _____
    A) Assembler B) Compiler   C) Editor   D) Linker.

136. Which of the following is specific to object oriented programming?
    A) Declare-Define-Use
    B) Public functions & Private variables
    C) Top down programming
    D) Function Calls.

137. Computer system consist of two major components. They are _____.
    A) Program & algorithm
    B) Hardware & software
    C) Hardware & program
    D) Instructions & Program.

138. The languages that favor human being are termed as_____
    A) social language
    B) classical language
    C) high-level language
    D) low level language.

139. The languages oriented to the machine are known as_____.
    A) Artificial language
    B) high level language
    C) low level language
    D) structured level language.

140. Which programming language is machine dependent?
    A) Machine level language
    B) Assembly level language
    C) High level language
    D) Both A and B

141. An assembler _____.
    A) translate a machine language code into an assembly language code
    B) translate an assembly language code into a machine language code
    C) translate an assembly language into high level language
    D) translate a machine level language into middle level language.

142. Machine language is in the form of
    A) All 0s   B) 1s and 0s   C) All 1s   D) None of these.

143. Almost every programming language has_____.
    A) mechanism for dynamically up-dating the storage
    B) symbolic names
    C) control structures
    D) all of the above.

144. BASIC stand for _____ .
    A) Beginner All Purpose Symbolic Instruction Code
    B) Formula translation
    C) Object oriented programming
    D) None of these.

145. Java was developed by_____
    A) AT&T
    B) Microsoft
    C) Sun Microsystems
    D) Redhat.

146. BASIC was developed in the year 1994 by _____ .
    A) Grace Hopper
    B) Dennis Ritche.
    C) John Backus
    D) John Kameny.

147. FORTRAN was developed by _____ .
    A) Grace Hopper
    B) Dennis Ritche
    C) John Backus
    D) James Gosling.

148. What is used to interpret the preprocessor directives?
    A) A Compiler
    B) An Interpretor
    C) A Pre processor
    D) None of the above.

149. All preprocessor directives are proceed _____
    A) Before compilation of the program
    B) After compilation
    C) During execution
    D) None of the above.

150. Machine languages are
    A) Third generation languages.
    B) First generation languages.
    C) Second generation languages.
    D) None of above.

151. Machine language is _____ .
    A) the language in which the machine can uderstood the program
    B) is the only language understood by the computer
    C) differs from one type of computer to another
    D) All of these.

152. 'C' can be used on
    A) Only MS-DOS operating system
    B) Only unix operating system
    C) Only WINDOWS operating system
    D) All of the above.

153. HTML is a type of _____.
   A) High level Language B) Low Level Language
   C) Symbolic language   D) Scripting language.

154. _____ is the first High Level Language to be implemented for personal computers
   A) BASIC   B) C   C) C++   D) JAVA

155. Allocation of memory to variables is carried by _____ when the program is executed
   A) Compiler   B) Translator
   C) Editor   D) Operating system.

156. An interpreter
   A) generates a permanent object code file
   B) does not generates an object code file
   C) allows to write code in high level language
   D) does not allows to write code in high level language.

157. Which of the following statement is wrong?
   A) Windows XP is an Operating System.
   B) Linux is owned and sold by the Microsoft Corporation.
   C) Photoshop is a graphical design tool by Adobe Photoshop.
   D) Linux is free open source software.

158. BASIC is _____ .
   A) High Level Language   B) Low Level Lang.
   C) Assembly Language   D) None of above.

159. LISP is
   A) Object oriented   B) List oriented
   C) Class oriented   D) All of the above.

160. Machine level language code is called
   A) Object Code   B) Source code
   C) Byte Code   D) None of Above.

161. The Computer can understand only _____ without the help of a language translator.
   A) English language   B) C language
   C) Machine language   D) Assembly language.

162. Which of the following is widely used language for scientific and engineering computation
    A) Cobol   B) Basic   C) Pascal   D) Fortran.
163. Which statement is valid about interpreter?
    A) Repeated interpretation is not necessary
    B) It translates one instruction at a time
    C) Object code is saved for future use
    D) All of the above.
164. Compiler bridges the semantic gap between a
    A) Programming language domain and execution domain
    B) Scope analysis and dynamic analysis
    C) Automatic allocation and program controlled allocation
    D) None of the above.
165. Which of the following is not a language for computer programming?
    A) Windows   B) Pascal   C) COBOL   D) All of these.
166. A browser is a software tool that helps
    A) Linking of application program modules
    B) Viewing the web pages
    C) Developing application programs
    D) Debugging of application software.
167. Which type of files are linked by a linker :
    A) Object Files   B) Executable Files
    C) Source Files   D) All Files.
168. This is a number crunching program. & still used by scientist because the language allows variables of any size up to the memory limit of the machine.
    A) FORTRAN   B) C   C) JAVA   D) ADA)
169. Which of the following languages is suited for business appilications?
    A) COBOL   B) PL/I
    C) Assembly   D) None of Above.
170. A complier is a_____ .
    A) Machine   B) Software
    C) part of machine   D) Hardware.

Unit 1 | 1.39

171. The other name for the scripting language is _____.
    A) Extension Language   B) Middle level language
    C) Low level language   D) natural Language.

172. A language translator that does not generate a permanent object code file is known as _____.
    A) Loader   B) Linker   C) Object file   D) Interpreter.

173. The 'C' language is a Case sensitive language. Validate this statement.
    A) The statement is correct
    B) The statement is wrong
    C) The statement is partially correct
    D) None of above options is applicable.

174. Which one of the following is not al program development tool ?
    A) Compiler   B) Linker   C) Virtual machine   D) Editor.

175. A Loader is a component of a _____ .
    A) Editor   B) Operating system
    C) Compiler   D) Debugger.

176. The fastest execution speed is achievable with the _____ language
    A) Machine-level   B) Assembly-level
    C) Low-level   D) High-level.

177. Assembly languages are High Level languages
    A) The statement is correct
    B) The statement is wrong
    C) The statement is partially correct
    D) None of above.

178. _____ is the quality of a Machine Language.
    A) Machine Independent
    B) Difficult to Program
    C) Easy to modify
    D) Not easily understood by the computer.

179. C++ is a _____ language.
    A) object oriented programming
    B) procedural programming
    C) functional programming
    D) logic programming.

180. Which of the following programming language is used for writing UNIX operating system ?
    A) FORTRAN   B) COBOL   C) Pascal   D) C)

181. A text editor is a _____ utility ?
    A) software
    B) hardware
    C) Both hardware and software
    D) none of the above.

182. Which of the following is not programming language?
    A) Low level
    B) Natural
    C) Scripting
    D) Assembly.

183. _____ is translated by the language processor
    A) input data
    B) Input and output data
    C) output data
    D) program code.

184. A machine language instruction has a two-part format. First part is_____ and second part is _____.
    A) OPCODE, OPERAND
    B) OPERAND, OPCODE
    C) OPERAND, DATA
    D) ADDRESS, OPERAND

185. What is the limitation of high level language?
    A) Lower efficiency
    B) Machine dependent
    C) Machine level coding
    D) None of the above.

186. Machine-level program is written in the form of _____.
    A) binary numbers
    B) hexadecimal numbers
    C) octal numbers
    D) none of these.

187. The Examples of the high level languages are _____.
    A) FORTRAN & Cobol
    B) basic & Pascal
    C) C,C++, Java, RPG, LISP SNOBOL
    D) all of the above.

188. Which of the following is true?
    A) C language is an object-oriented language
    B) C language is a procedural language
    C) C language is functional language
    D) C language is a machine-level language.

189. What is a compiler?
    A) A compiler is a special program that processes the program and loads it into the memory
    B) A compiler is a special program that processes statements written in a particular programming language and turns them into assembly/intermidiate language
    C) A compiler is a special program that combines different object modules to form an executable program.
    D) Compiler is a computer program that executes, or performs, instructions written in a computer programming language.

190. The language like BASIC, C, FORTAN & PASCAL are the examples of _____
    A) Low level languages   B) High level languages
    C) Machine level languages   D) None of the above.

191. An operating system utility that copies program from a storage device to the main memory, where it can be executed is know as a _____
    A) Linker   B) Loader   C) compiler   D) interpreter.

192. A Program is compiled using a special utility commonly called as a _____.
    A) Compiler   B) Linker   C) Assembler   D) Loader.

193. A _____ is the utility, which is used to trace and identify flow of control during execution of a program.
    A) Compiler   B) Debugger   C) Interpreter   D) Loader.

194. Which of the following is used for internet based appilications?
    A) C   B) C++   C) Java   D) Prolog.

195. Examples of the Language processor is / are _____.
    A) assembler   B) complier
    C) interpreter   D) All of the above.

196. Which of the following high level languages follows object oriented approach?
    A) COBOL   B) LISP   C) BASIC   D) JAVA

197. _____ is used to create web pages.
    A) C++   B) HTML   C) C language   D) Java script.

198. A language, which allows instructions and storage locations to be represented by symbols, is called an _____ language.
    A) Machine   B) Binary   C) High level   D) None.

FPL – I ENGG. (F.E. SEM. I)   INTRODUCTION

199. The file created from the _____ is known as object module
   A) linker   B) loader
   C) compiler   D) none of the above.

200. Machine and Assembly Language are often referred to as _____.
   A) low level language   B) middle level language
   C) high level language   D) Object oriented language.

201. The Assembly languages are machine dependent languages. Validate this statement.
   A) The statement is correct
   B) The statement is wrong
   C) The statement is partially correct
   D) None of above options is applicable.

202. Assemblers, compilers and interpreters are also referred to as _____.
   A) Processors   B) Programs
   C) Language   D) Language Processors.

203. Which of the following editor is most often used to edit the ` C ` programs?
   A) TURBO C editor   B) DOS editor
   C) Kawa editor   D) Jcreator.

204. The task of combining all the object program files modules of a program and then converting them in to a final executable program is done by _____ utility.
   A) compiler   B) assembler
   C) Linker   D) Interpreter.

205. A _____ is the language prefered to write a program.
   A) Machine   B) Assembly   C) High-level   D) English.

206. After Compiling process, a source program is converted into a _____.
   A) object program   B) text program
   C) Executable program   D) Assemble Program.

207. An Interpreter translates and executes the program instructions _____.
   A) all together   B) onces for all
   C) statement by statement   D) none of these.

208. Pascal programs starts with the keyword _____
   A) Program   B) Begin   C) Var   D) Procedure.

Unit 1 | 1.43

209. _____ translates source code one line at a time
    A) Compiler   B) Interpreter   C) Linker   D) Loader.

210. Which of the following statement is correct as far as comparison of an interpreter and a compiler is concerned?
    A) they are slower than compliers   B) faster than compliers
    C) same speed as compliers   D) none of these.

211. COBOL stands for _____
    A) COMMON OBJETC BUSINESS ORIENTED LANGUAGE
    B) COMPUTER OBJECT BUSINESS ORIENTED LANGUAGE
    C) COMMON OBJECT BROKER ORIENTED LANGUAGE
    D) COMPUTER OBJECT BUSINESS ORIENTED LANGUAGE.

Documentation

212. In a 'C' language program , which form of documentation is used ?
    A) User manual   B) System manual
    C) Comments   D) Indentation

213. User manual should include _____ .
    A) Total number of source code files present in the system
    B) A guide explaining how to install, run and configure the system
    C) Both A and B
    D) None of the above

214. Documentation is used for easy understanding of_____
    A) Program s logic   B) Pseudocode
    C) Instructions   D) None of above

215. Which of the following forms a part of software documentation?
    A) Comments within programs   B) User manual
    C) System manual   D) All of the above

216. Setup and operational details of every program are available in _____
    A) System manual   B) User manual
    C) All Of the Above   D) None of the above

217. Comments are written using the _____ .
    A) General English Statements
    B) Assembly Language Statements
    C) Higher Level Language Statements
    D) Block Of Code

218. A system manual contains _____
    A) input requirements, forms, type of output required, flowcharts, control procedure
    B) information about OS
    C) manual of computer systems
    D) multimedia information

219. _____ do not contain any program logic and are ignored by language processor
    A) Protocols   B) Loops
    C) Comments   D) None of the above

220. Documentation is carried out in_____ phase.
    A) maintenance   B) testing
    C) system requirement D) implementation

221. Comments are _____
    A) Executable statements   B) Non executable statements
    C) Assignment statements   D) InputOutput statements

222. Documentation is any communicable material such as text, video, audio, etc, or combinations thereof which _____
    A) Explain some attributes of an object, system or procedure
    B) Are in books or computer readable file formats
    C) Describe the structure and components, or on the other hand, operation, of a systemproduct.
    D) All of above

223. Consider the following statements(a) Indentation makes programs more readable and simpler to understand(b) Indentation is compulsory while writing a program.Which of the following option is correct.
    A) Only(a) is true   B) Only(b) is true
    C) Both(a) and (b) are true D) Both (a) and (b) are false

224. How will you write comment in a ` C ` Program
    A) /   B) // //   C) /* */   D) /*

225. Documentation standards use _____ .
    A) Hungarian notations   B) Comments
    C) Function description   D) All above

226. What does user manual provide?
    A) Help for developer
    B) Help for end user
    C) Help for tester
    D) Help for analyst

227. Which of the following is generally used for documentation?
    A) Comments   B) Variables   C) Datatypes   D) Functions

228. _____ also specifies the information about the security measures for using the software.
    A) Program Messages
    B) user manual
    C) system manual
    D) comments

229. User manual are used for _____
    A) modifying the program
    B) maintaining a program
    C) to know the operational details of program
    D) None of above

230. _____ makes software easier to modify and adapt in future
    A) Proper documentation
    B) Flowchart
    C) Pseudocode
    D) Algorithm

231. The comments can be written in a program _____.
    A) within declarative statements
    B) within functions
    C) for any statement
    D) All of the above

232. System manual consists of_____
    A) Problem statements
    B) Detailed system flow
    C) Source listing of programs
    D) All of the above.

233. Block of comments is shown using the _____ symbols.
    A) /* /*   B) */ */   C) /* */   D) */ //*

234. Comments are helpful because _____ .
    A) It helps us to find out errors in program
    B) It helps us know the program execution time
    C) It helps us to understand source code
    D) It increases the performance of the code

235. Which of the following is a type of documentation?
    A) Comments   B) System Manual
    C) User Manual   D) All
236. Multiline comments in C are _____ .
    A) //   B) //* *//   C) /% %/   D) /* */
237. The process of collecting, organizing & maintaining a complete record of development of programs is called as _____.
    A) Testing   B) Documentation
    C) Debugging   D) Coding
238. Installation describes _____
    A) How to write the program   B) How to use the program
    C) How to install the program   D) How to read the program
239. Which of the followings is not a form of documentation?
    A) user manual   B) comments
    C) log books   D) system manual
240. System documentation includes _____
    A) Requirements Documents   B) System & Program Architecture
    C) Program Source Code   D) All Above
241. Documentation is needed because it _____
    A) is easier to understand the logic of program
    B) makes software easier to modify
    C) helps greatly while troubleshooting for errors
    D) All of the above
242. Commonly used form of documentation are _____
    A) only manual
    B) only comments
    C) user manual, system manual and comments
    D) None of the above
243. Indentation is generally only of use to the _____
    A) Programmers   B) Compiler
    C) Interpreters   D) Assemblers
244. Program documentation is used to _____
    A) Increase throughput   B) Increase maintainability
    C) Increase security   D) None of above

FPL – I ENGG. (F.E. SEM. I)   INTRODUCTION

245. Common types of computer hardware software documentation include _____
   A) Online help, FAQs   B) user guide
   C) Both A and B   D) None of above.

246. In which form of documentation System flow charts and program flow charts are included?
   A) Comments   B) User Manual
   C) System Manual   D) Code

247. What do you mean by documentation standards?
   A) Process of writing programs
   B) Rules and regulations about how documentation is to be performed
   C) Process of drawing flowcharts
   D) Proces of writing algorithms

248. _____ is primarily developed for end user.
   A) System manual   B) Quality Manual
   C) User manual   D) None of these

Answers

1.	B	2.	D	3.	C	4.	A	5.	B
6.	B	7.	D	8.	A	9.	A	10.	A
11.	D	12.	D	13.	C	14.	B	15.	A
16.	C	17.	C	18.	B	19.	D	20.	C
21.	C	22.	D	23.	C	24.	D	25.	A
26.	A	27.	D	28.	B	29.	D	30.	A
31.	C	32.	A	33.	A	34.	D	35.	A
36.	D	37.	A	38.	C	39.	C	40.	D
41.	B	42.	C	43.	B	44.	B	45.	B
46.	D	47.	C	48.	B	49.	A	50.	C
51.	A	52.	C	53.	B	54.	A	55.	D
56.	D	57.	C	58.	C	59.	A	60.	D
61.	B	62.	D	63.	A	64.	B	65.	A

66.	D	67.	D	68.	A	69.	D	70.	C
71.	C	72.	D	73.	B	74.	A	75.	D
76.	B	77.	C	78.	B	79.	C	80.	B
81.	B	82.	B	83.	C	84.	A	85.	B
86.	C	87.	B	88.	B	89.	B	90.	C
91.	C	92.	B	93.	B	94.	B	95.	B
96.	D	97.	A	98.	A	99.	C	100.	A
101.	B	102.	D	103.	A	104.	B	105.	C
106.	A	107.	A	108.	C	109.	C	110.	A
111.	D	112.	D	113.	A	114.	A	115.	D
116.	D	117.	A	118.	A	119.	B	120.	C
121.	B	122.	A	123.	B	124.	A	125.	B
126.	B	127.	A	128.	D	129.	B	130.	D
131.	C	132.	B	133.	A	134.	C	135.	D
136.	B	137.	B	138.	C	139.	C	140.	D
141.	B	142.	B	143.	D	144.	A	145.	C
146.	D	147.	C	148.	C	149.	A	150.	B
151.	D	152.	D	153.	D	154.	A	155.	D
156.	B	157.	B	158.	A	159.	B	160.	A
161.	C	162.	D	163.	B	164.	A	165.	A
166.	B	167.	A	168.	A	169.	A	170.	B
171.	A	172.	D	173.	A	174.	C	175.	B
176.	A	177.	B	178.	B	179.	A	180.	D
181.	A	182.	B	183.	D	184.	A	185.	D
186.	A	187.	D	188.	B	189.	B	190.	B
191.	B	192.	A	193.	B	194.	C	195.	D
196.	D	197.	B	198.	C	199.	C	200.	A
201.	A	202.	D	203.	A	204.	C	205.	C

206.	A	207.	C	208.	A	209.	B	210.	A
211.	A	212.	C	213.	B	214.	A	215.	B
216.	D	217.	A	218.	A	219.	C	220.	D
221.	B	222.	D	223.	A	224.	C	225.	D
226.	B	227.	A	228.	B	229.	C	230.	A
231.	D	232.	B	233.	C	234.	C	235.	D
236.	D	237.	B	238.	C	239.	C	240.	D
241.	D	242.	C	243.	A	244.	B	245.	C
246.	C	247.	B	248.	C				

INTRODUCTION

Syllabus

Algorithm. Advantages of Generalized Algorithms. How to make Algorithms Generalized. Avoiding infinite loops in Algorithms – By Counting, By using a Sentinel Value. Different ways of Representing an Algorithm – As a Program, As a Flowchart, As a Pseudo code; Need for Planning a Program before Coding. Program planning tools – Flowcharts, Structure charts, Pseudo codes.

Importance of use of indentation in programming. Structured programming concepts – Need for careful use of "Go to" statements, How all programs can be written using Sequence Logic, Selection Logic and Iteration (or looping) Logic, functions.

2.1 Algorithm

A finite set of instructions, which if followed, accomplishes a particular task or it is a description of a logical order of actions.

Characteristics of Algorithm

1. **Input :** An algorithm has zero or more but only, finite number of inputs.
2. **Output:** An algorithm must produce at least one output.
3. **Definiteness:** Each instruction must be clear and unambiguous.
4. **Finiteness:** An algorithm must have a finite number of instructions, i.e. it always terminates. This is one of the most important differences between an algorithm and a program. An algorithm always terminates while a program may or may not terminate.
5. **Effectiveness:** Every instruction of an algorithm must be feasible. It should be possible to carry out the instructions of the algorithm.

Thus, an algorithm can be formally described as a well-ordered finite collection of unambiguous and effectively computable operations that when executed produces a result.

Problem definition: Given a number 'N' different than '0', we want to determine if it is positive or negative. The algorithm block in the following figure identifies whether the input given is positive or negative.

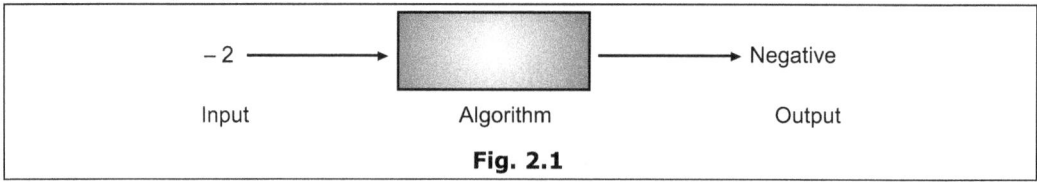

Fig. 2.1

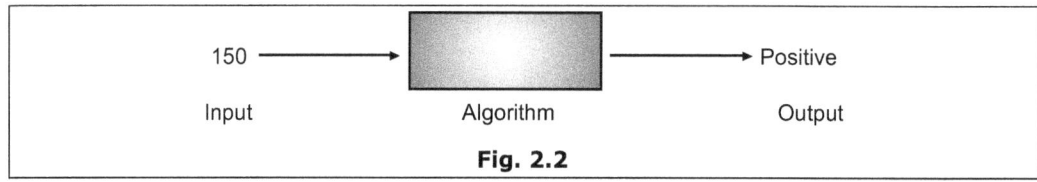

Fig. 2.2

Algorithm for Addition of Two numbers

Step 1: Start

Step 2: Accept two numbers in variable A & B

Step 3: Perform the addition (A+B) and store in the third variable(say C) i.e. C=A+B

Step 4: Print the value of C

Step 5: Stop

2.2 Generalized Algorithm

A generalized algorithm is an algorithm which defines a set of steps for solving a number of problems of similar type.

For example, we can design an algorithm to find the area of problems of similar type or to find the area of any two-dimensional geometric figure which can find area of line, circle, rectangle etc.

2.2.1 Advantages of Generalized Algorithms

- ➢ **Prescriptive Limitations:** Generalized algorithms do not restrict the algorithm to the programmers knowledge for a particular language.

- **Solution-Centric:** Generalized algorithms help to focus solely on the solution to your problem
- **Assumption Avoidance:** Using generalized logic helps you avoid a variety of assumptions.
- **Non-specialist Friendly:** Even if you don't have knowledge of the implementation details of an algorithm you may understand the basic concept with the help of a generalized algorithm.

2.3 Avoiding Infinite Loops in algorithms

An **infinite loop** or **endless loop** or **unproductive loop** is a sequence of instructions in a computer program which loops endlessly, either due to:

- The loop having no terminating condition **or**
- Having a condition that can never be met **or**
- A condition that causes the loop to start over.

Infinite loops usually cause the program to consume all available processor time, but can usually be terminated by the user.

Example in C

```c
#include <stdio.h>
main()
{
    while(1)
    {
        printf("Infinite Loop\n");
    }
}
```

This is a loop that will print "Infinite Loop" without halting.

This happens when the condition will never be met, due to some inherent characteristic of the loop.

2.4 Methods to avoid Infinite Loops

Following are the methods to avoid infinite loops.

Repetitions are controlled by

1. Counter
2. Using a Sentinel value

2.4.1 Controlling loops by Using a Counter

A counter is a variable that can be used to prespecify the number of times the statements or instructions inside the loop will be executed.

Example:

```
start
    num count=0
    while count<4
        {
         print "Hello"
         count=count+1
        }
    end while
stop
```

Explanation:

In the above program, the variable count is initialized to 0. Using a while loop the count is incremented till 3 and Hello gets printed 4 times as the count increments from 0 to 3.

These actions make a WHILE loop end correctly:

- Loop control variable is initialized
    - Prior to entering the loop
- Loop control variable is tested
    - If result is true, loop body entered
- Loop control variable altered by:
    - Incrementing the count
    - Decrementing the count

Following is the flowchart for the above program.

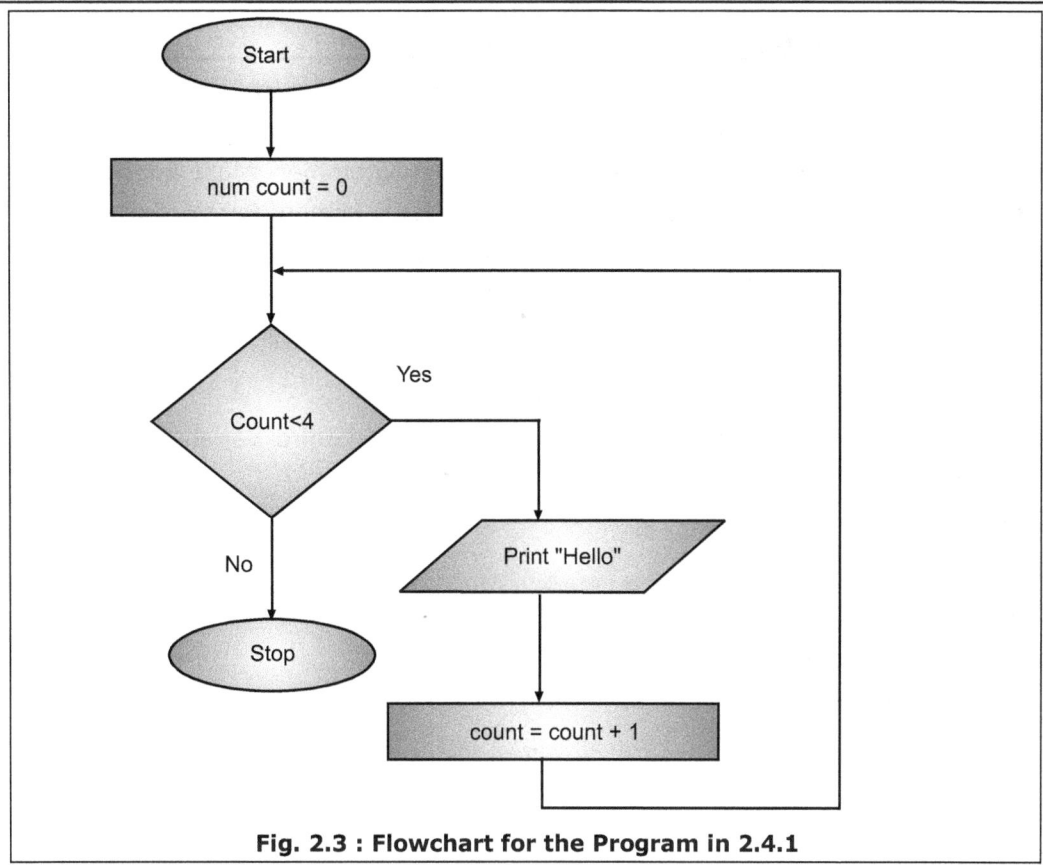

Fig. 2.3 : Flowchart for the Program in 2.4.1

2.4.2 By Using a Sentinel Value

Sentinel value is used for controlling indefinite loops. It is a response or a signal to end a loop. In computer programming, a sentinel value is also referred to as a **flag value.** The sentinel value makes it possible to detect the end of the data when no other means to do so is provided

Example:

2.5 Representing an Algorithm

There are number of ways to represent an algorithm.

An algorithm can be represented using:

1. A Program
2. A Flowchart
3. A Pseudo code

2.5.1 Representing an Algorithm as a Program

An algorithm is a set of instructions written in plain English language which can be represented as a Program. To represent an algorithm as a program we can make use of several programming languages which a programmer might know. We can make use of all High Level languages like C, C++,Java, Python, Pascal, Fortran etC)

Consider an algorithm for addition of two numbers

Step 1: Start

Step 2 : Declare variables A, B, C

Step 3: Accept two numbers in variable A & B

Step 4: Perform the addition (A+B) and store in the third variable(say C) i.e.
C=A+B

Step 5: Print the value of C

Step 6: Stop

C Program for the above algorithm.

```c
#include<stdio.h>
#include<conio.h>
void main()
{
    int A, B, C;
    clrscr();
    printf("\nEnter two numbers A and B:");
    scanf(" %d%d",&A,&B);
    C=A+B;
    printf("Addition=%d",C);
    getch();
}
```

The above program adds A and B and store the addition in variable C and finally prints the value of C) The same algorithm can be represented in various Programming Languages .

2.5.2 Representing an Algorithm as a Flowchart

A flowchart is **a diagrammatic representation** of an algorithm. After an algorithm has been written, we convert it into a flowchart. It makes use of certain standard symbols. It is a pictorial step by step guide that a programmer uses when planning the solution to a problem.

Given below are some symbols which are used for constructing a Flowchart.

Sr. No.	Symbol	Function
1.	(oval)	**The Terminal Block:** It is used to indicate the beginning or end of flowchart.
2.	(parallelogram)	**The Input/output Symbol:** All instructions used to read values or display the answers are included in these type of symbols.
3.	(rectangle)	**The Process Symbol:** All calculations and formulas are included within a rectangle
4.	(rectangle with double vertical lines)	**Predefined Process Symbol:** Indicate a set of steps that combine to create a sub-process that is defined elsewhere, often on another page of the same drawing.
5.	(diamond)	**The Decision Box:** Whenever a decision is to be taken depending on a certain condition being met or not, a decision box is useD)
6.	(arrows)	**The Flow Lines:** These indicate the direction of the logic flow.
7.	(circle)	**The Connector:** Whenever we are not able to complete our flowchart on the same page, we make use of what is called a connector. It is used to connect to different parts of a flowchart.

Fig. 2.4 : Symbols used for constructing Flowchart

Example 1:

Consider an algorithm for calculating the area and perimeter of a rectangle.

Step 1: Start

Step 2 : Declare variables Length, Breadth, Area and Perimeter.

Step 3: Accept/Read Length and Breadth.

Step 4: Calculate the area of rectangle with the formula Area=Length*Breadth.

Step 5: Calculate the perimeter of rectangle with the formula 2*(Length*Breadth).

Step 6: Print the Area of the rectangle.

Step 7: Print the Perimeter of the rectangle.

Step 8: Stop

Flowchart :

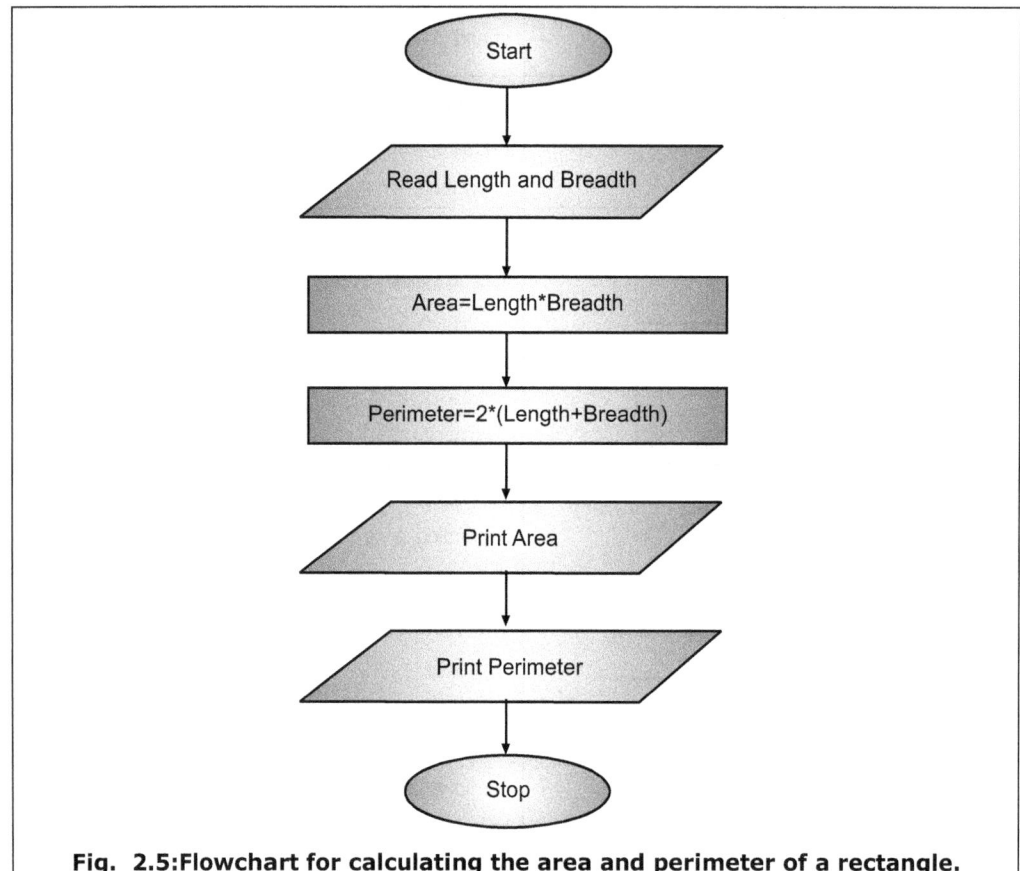

Fig. 2.5: Flowchart for calculating the area and perimeter of a rectangle.

Example 2:

Consider an algorithm to print whether a student has passed or failed depending on the marks he/she has scored

Step 1: Start

Step 2 : Declare variables Name and Marks.

Step 3: Accept/Read Name and Marks.

Step 4: Check the condition whether the marks are greater or equal to 40.

Step 5: If Marks>=40, print Name and PASSED)\

Step 6: If Marks<40, print Name and FAILED)
Step 7: Stop
Flowchart:

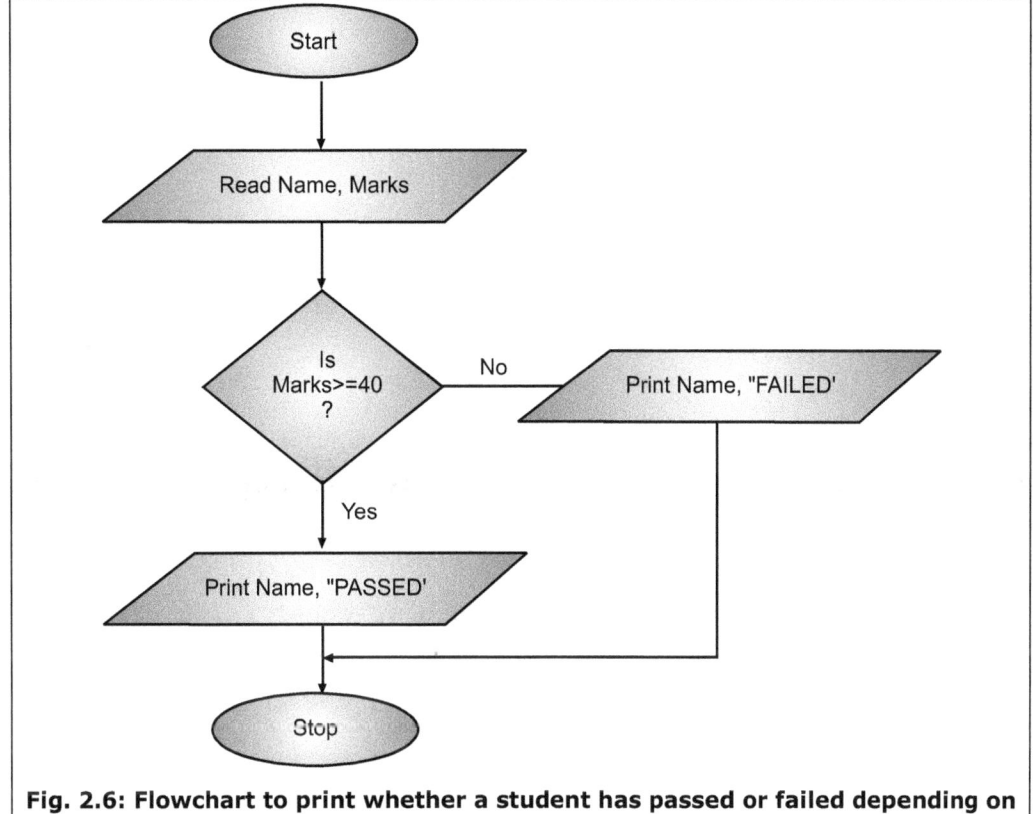

Fig. 2.6: Flowchart to print whether a student has passed or failed depending on the marks he/she has scored

In the above example, the decision to declare a student as passed or failed depends on the marks secured. Hence, we make use of the decision box, which very clearly indicates the action to be taken in both the cases(whether the marks are greater than or equal to 40).

2.5.3 Representing an Algorithm as a Pseudo Code

The prefix pseudo means "fake" or "false". Pseudo code, therefore, literally means "fake code" that is, not the code that is actually entered into the computer. It is more precise in representing logic than the regular English, but does not follow a specific programming language syntax. Pseudo code typically omits details that are not essential for human understanding of the algorithm, such as variable declarations, system-specific code and some subroutines.

Example 1:

Pseudo code for calculating and displaying the area and perimeter of rectangle.

```
START
      READ Length
      READ Breadth
            Calculate Area
                  Area=Length*Breadth
                  Calculate Perimeter
                  Perimeter=2*(Length*Breadth)
      Display Area
      Display Perimeter
END
```

Example 2:

Pseudo code for printing whether a student has passed or failed depending on his marks.

```
START
      IF student's grade is greater than or equal to 40
            Print "passed"
      ELSE
            Print "failed"
END
```

2.6 Program Planning

- Creating a program is third stage or coding stage of software.
- Before coding we need to plan and design the program.
- It is very important to plan before building or implementing any program.

2.6.1 Need of Program Planning or Designing

- Planning helps us to get an overview of the whole program.
- Planning or designing becomes a major guideline for the developer in developing the program.
- While building a program we should follow all the steps of software development cycle.
- Major errors can be detected at early stages.

2.6.2 Program Planning Tools

There are different tools used to plan or design programs. Few of them are listed below:

(I)   **Flowcharts**
(II) **Pseudo codes**
(III) **Structure charts**

(I) Flowcharts

- Flowcharts represent the flow of the algorithm.
- Specific shapes are used to represent the steps in an algorithm.
- Using these shapes makes the representation structures and easy to understand
- The arrows connecting the symbols, called flow lines, show the progression in which the steps take place.
- It gives graphical representation of the program.

Example 1:

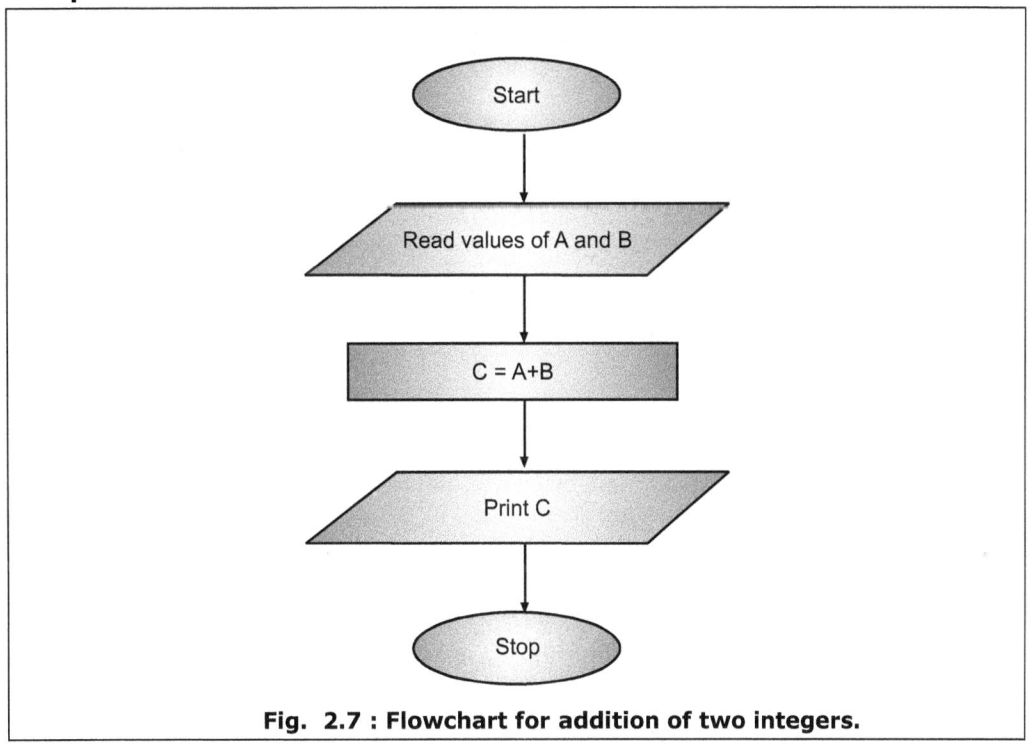

Fig. 2.7 : Flowchart for addition of two integers.

Example 2:

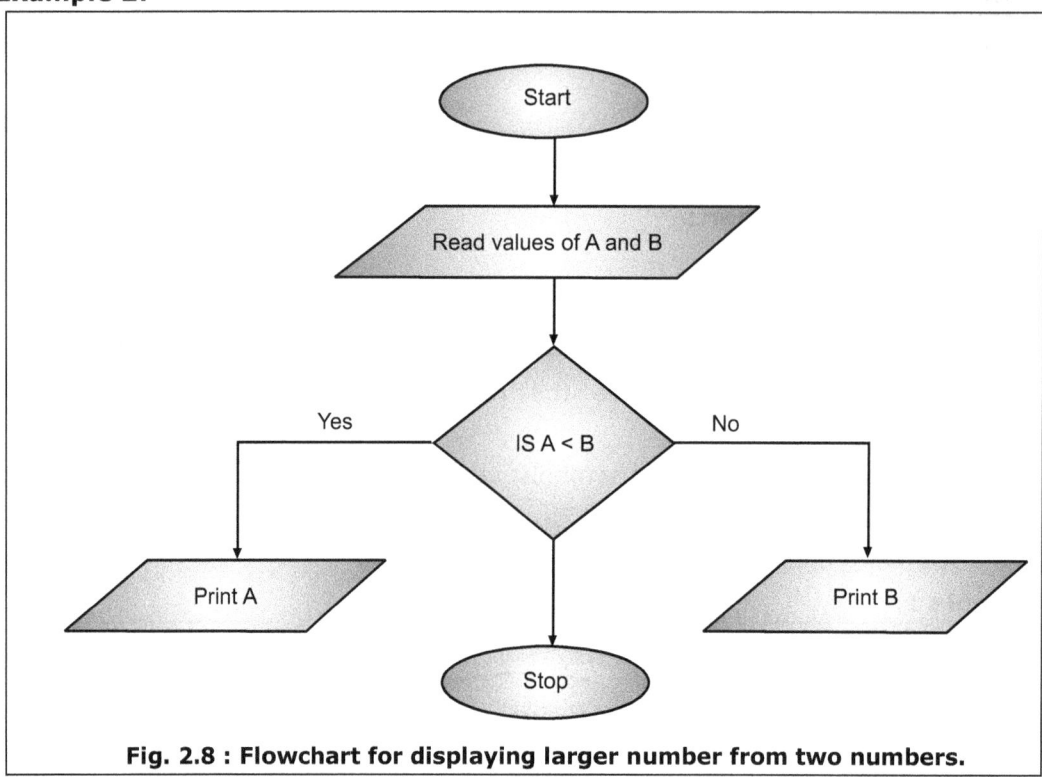

Fig. 2.8 : Flowchart for displaying larger number from two numbers.

Advantages of Flowchart:

- **Communication:** Flowcharts are better way of communicating the logic of a system.
- **Effective Analysis:** With the help of flowchart, problem can be analyzed in more effective way.
- **Efficient Coding:** The flowcharts act as a guide or blueprint during the systems analysis and program development phase.
- **Proper Debugging:** The flowchart helps in debugging process.

Disadvantages of Flowchart

- **Alterations and Modifications:** If alterations are required the flowchart may require re-drawing completely.
- **Reproduction:** As the flowchart symbols cannot be typed, reproduction of flowchart becomes a problem.

- **Complex logic:** Sometimes, the program logic is quite complicated In that case, flowchart becomes complex and clumsy.

(II) Pseudo codes

- Pseudo code means instructions written in any ordinary **natural language.**
- Instead of symbols as in flowchart it uses **structure** which resembles computer instructions
- Pseudo code emphasizes on design of program , it is also called as PDL (**Program Design Language**)

Example: Pseudo code for displaying larger number from two numbers.

```
START
   IF  A<B
      Print "A"
   ELSE
      Print "B"
END
```

Advantages of Pseudocode

- It is very easy to represent the program.
- This tool is used for generic representation of program.
- Impose increased discipline on the process of documenting detailed design.

Disadvantages of Pseudocode

- Create an additional level of documentation to maintain.
- Introduce error possibilities in translating to code.
- Complex programs can become confusing as general language is used

(III) Structure charts

- Structure charts show how the different parts of a program relate to each other.
- Structure chart show structure of program than details.
- They are generally used in large programs where programs are divided into many modules.
- Hierarchy charts may also be called
    1. Structure charts
    2. HIPO(Hierarchy plus Input-Process-Output) charts

3. Top-down charts
4. VTOC(Visual Table of Contents) charts

Example:

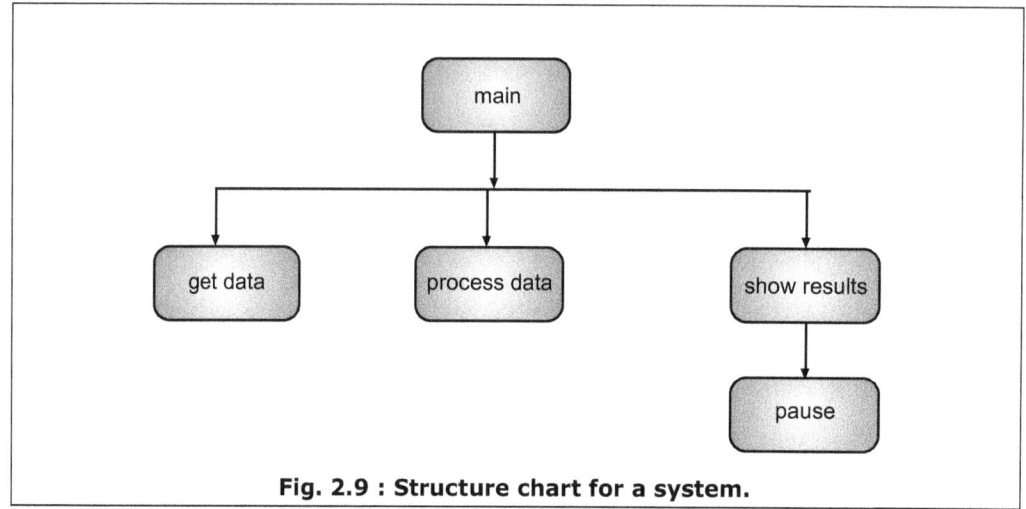

Fig. 2.9 : Structure chart for a system.

2.6.3 Advantages of Program Planning Tools

- Flowchart is related to internal logic and flow of control from one statement to another in a program. So this makes the program tracing easy thus making programs easy to debug.
- Pseudo code illustrate the various steps in easy to understand languages so it also makes the problem easy to write, read and understand thus making the resulting code simple and easy to read
- Structure chart represents the top down design of the problem steps of the process. It makes the program easy to read and understand before actually designing the code.

2.7 Importance of use of Indentation of Programming

In computer programming languages, indentation is used to format program source code to improve readability. Indentation is generally only of use to programmers. Compilers and interpreters rarely care how much whitespace is present in between programming statements. Indenting is adding spaces/tabs in front of 'blocks' of code (such as If-End If), so that it is easier for us and other people to see how the code flows.

Example: Program with indentation and without indentation.

Program with Indentation	Program without Indentation

`#include<stdio.h>`
 `#include<conio.h>`
 `void main()`
 `{`
    `int A, B;`
    `clrscr();`
    `printf("\nEnter two numbers A and B:");`
    `scanf(" %d%d",&A,&B);`
    `if(A<B)`
    `{`
      `printf("A is less than B");`
    `}`
    `else`
    `{`
      `printf("A is greater than B");`
    `}`
    `getch();`
 `}`
	`#include<stdio.h>`
	 `#include<conio.h>`
	 `void main()`
	 `{`
	 `int A, B;`
	 `clrscr();`
	 `printf("\nEnter two numbers A and B:");`
	 `scanf(" %d%d",&A,&B);`
	 `if(A<B)`
	 `{`
	 `printf("A is lwss than B ");`
	 `}`
	 `else`
	 `{`
	 `printf("A is greater than B");`
	 `}`
	 `getch();`
	 `}`

Advantages of Indentation:

1. Increases the readability of the program.
2. Helps to locate errors easily in a program.
3. We can immediately ignore chunks of the code that aren't relevant to what we are currently doing.
4. Helps in find out beginning and end of section of code(block of statements).

2.8 Structured Programming Concepts

Structured programming is a method used to design and code programs in a systematic, organized manner. It emerged in the year 1960 as a programming paradigm, aimed on improving the clarity, quality, and development time of a computer program by making extensive use of subroutines, block structures and looping structures. Use of "Go to" statement is discouraged which is both difficult to follow and maintain.

2.8.1 "Go to" statement

The **goto** statement is used to alter the normal sequence of program execution by transferring control to some other part of the program unconditionally. Using a goto statement in a program is not considered as a good programming practice. In its general form, the goto statement is written as *goto label;* where the label is an identifier that is used to label the target statement to which the control is transferred Control may be transferred to anywhere within the current function. The target statement must be labeled, and a colon must follow the label. Thus the target statement will appear as

label: statement;

Each labeled statement within the function must have a unique label, i.e., no two statements can have the same label.

Example: For go to statement

```
#include <stdio.h>
#include <conio.h>
int main()
{
    int n = 0;
    loop:
    printf("\n%d", n);
    n++;
    if (n<10)
        {
            goto loop;
        }
    getch();
    return 0;
}
```

You can see in the given example, we want to display the numbers from 0 to 9. For this, we have defined the label statement **loop** above the **goto** statement. The given program declares a variable n initialized to zero. The **n++** increments the value of n till the loop reaches 10. Then on declaring the **goto** statement, it jumps to the label statement and prints the value of n.

Need for careful use of "Go to" statements

- A goto statement causes your program to unconditionally transfer control to the statement associated with the label specified on the goto statement.
- The goto statement can interfere with the normal sequence of processing, it makes a program more difficult to read and maintain.
- Often, a break statement, a continue statement, or a function call can eliminate the need for a goto statement.
- If an active block is exited using a goto statement, any local variables are destroyed when control is transferred from that block.
- You cannot use a goto statement to jump over initializations.
- A goto statement is allowed to jump within the scope of a variable length array, but not pass any declarations of objects with variably modified types.

2.9 How all programs can be written using Sequence Logic, Selection Logic and Iteration (or looping Logic)

- **Sequence logic** is a logic which describes a sequence of actions that a program carries out one after another, unconditionally.
- **Selection** is the program construct that allows a program to choose between different actions. It allows for alternative paths to be taken through a program.
- **Iteration logic** is a logic in which programmer specifies an action to be repeated while some condition remains true.

2.9.1 Sequence Logic

- Statements are executed one by one until the end of the program is reached
- A group of statements that are executed sequentially which is usually grouped (bracketed) by { } is known as Compound Statements.

2.9.1.1 Basic structure of sequence logic

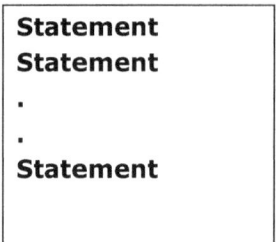

2.9.1.2 Generalized Flowchart for Sequence Logic

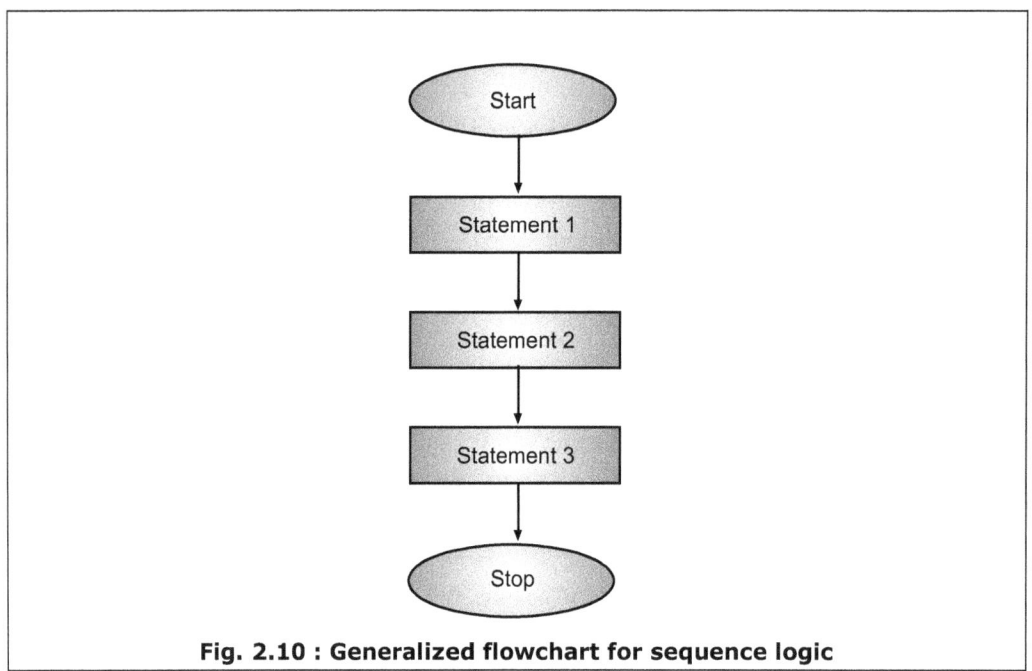

Fig. 2.10 : Generalized flowchart for sequence logic

2.9.1.3 Example of Sequence Logic

Step 1: Start

Step 2 : Declare variables P, R, N and I.

Step 3: Accept/Read P, R, N and I .

Step 4: Calculate the Interest with the formula I=P*R*N/100 .

Step 5: Print the value of I.

Step 6: Stop

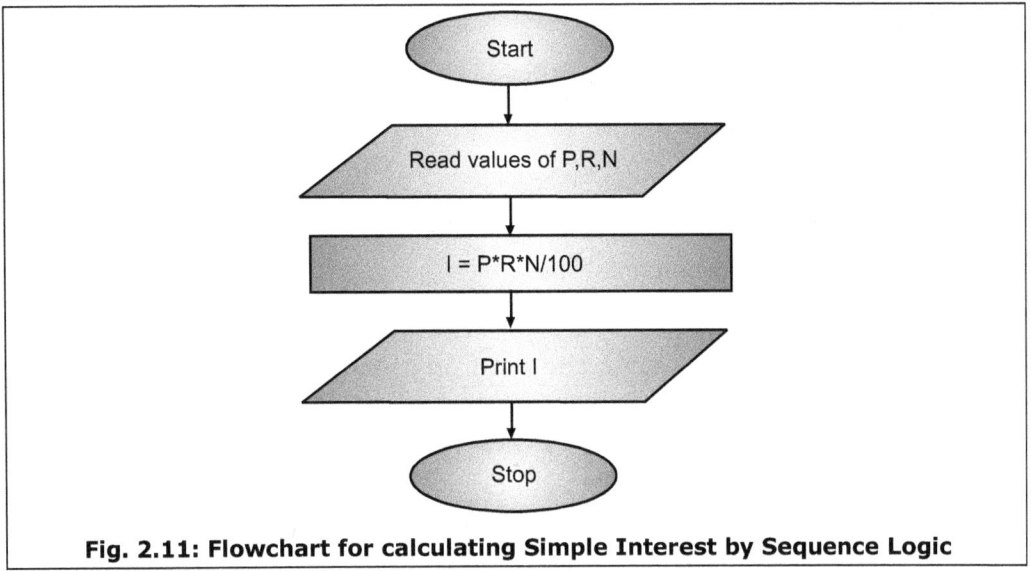

Fig. 2.11: Flowchart for calculating Simple Interest by Sequence Logic

2.9.2 Selection Logic

- In selection structure, the program is executed based upon the given condition.
- Only instructions that satisfy the given condition are executed
- There are different types of selection structure:
    1. if
       One alternative
    2. if...else
       Two alternatives
    3. nested if..else
       Multiple alternatives
    4. switch
       Multiple alternatives

2.9.2.1 Basic Structure of Selection Logic

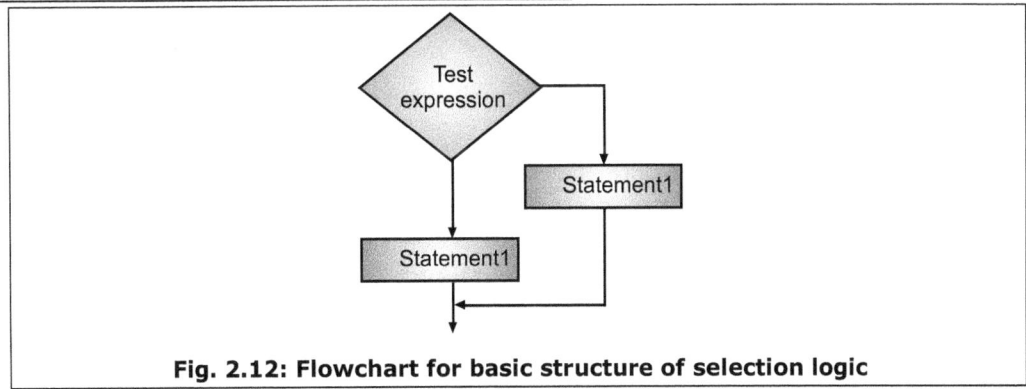

Fig. 2.12: Flowchart for basic structure of selection logic

2.9.2.2 Example for Selection Logic

Step 1: Start

Step 2 : Declare and accept variable N .

Step 3: Check for the condition if(N%2==0).

Step 4: if(N%2==0)...print entered number is Even.

Step 5: else print entered number is OdD)

Step 6: Stop.

Flowchart for displaying whether the entered number is even or odd

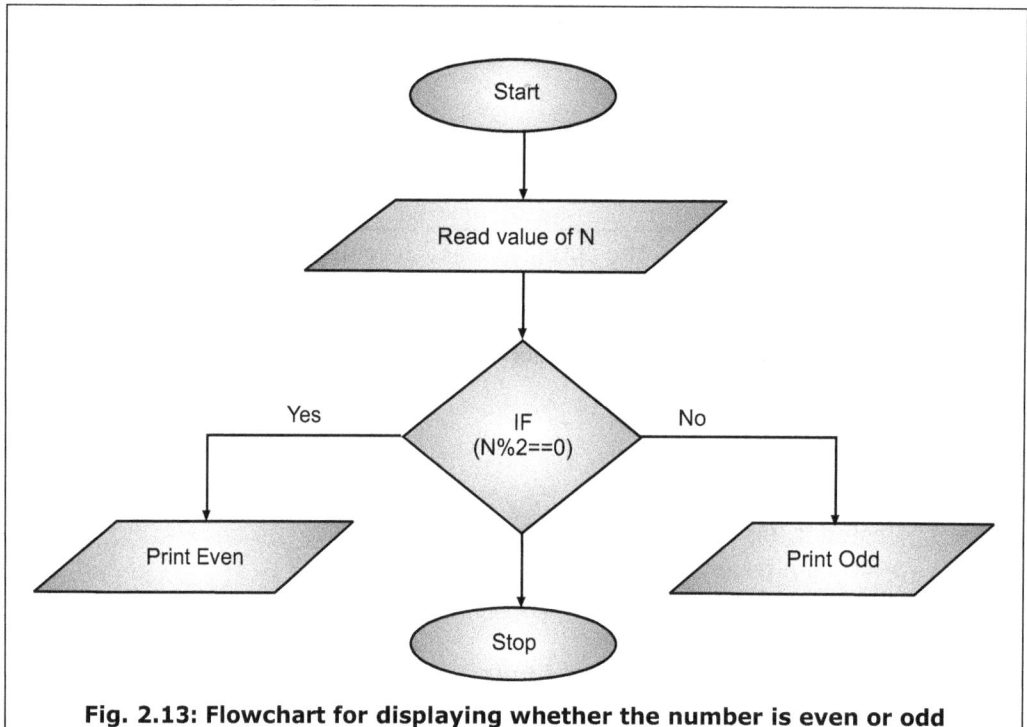

Fig. 2.13: Flowchart for displaying whether the number is even or odd

2.9.3 Iteration (Repetition) Logic

- Used to execute a number of statements from the program more than one time without having to write the statements multiple times.
- Two designs of loop :
    1. To execute a number of instructions from the program for a finite, pre-determined number of time (Counter controlled loop)

2. To execute a number of instructions from the program indefinitely until the user tells it to stop or a special condition is met (Sentinel-controlled loop)

- There are 3 types of iteration loops in C:
    1. while
    2. do...while
    3. for

2.9.3.1 Basic Structure of Selection Logic

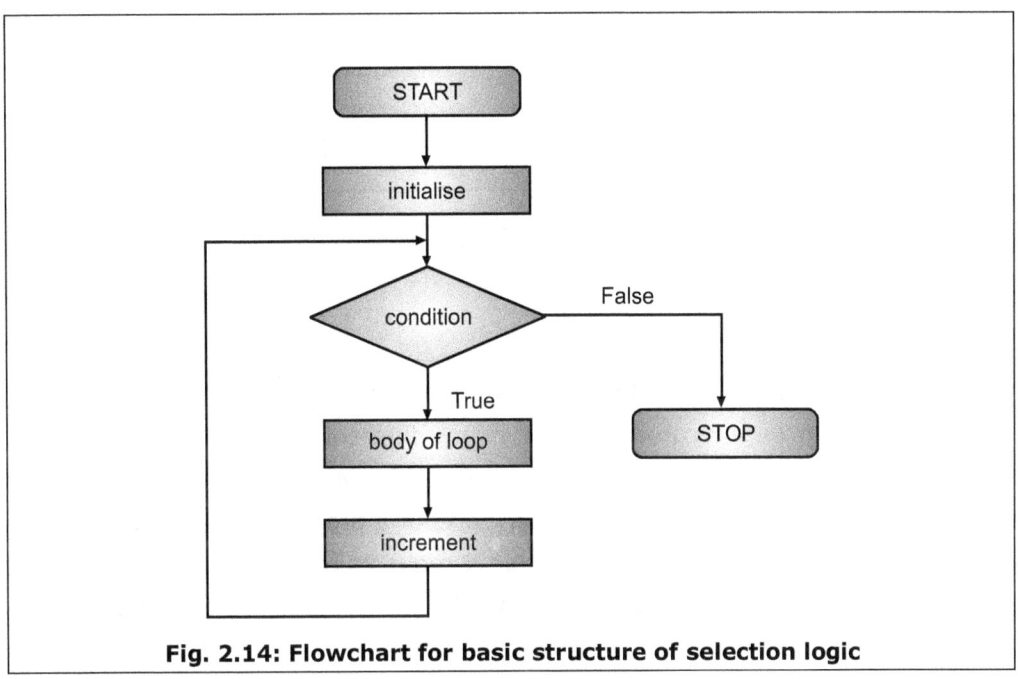

Fig. 2.14: Flowchart for basic structure of selection logic

Example for iteration logic:

Step 1: Start

Step 2 : Declare variable i and accept variable n .

Step 3: Initialize variable i to 1

Step 4: Check for the condition for(n=1,n<10;n++).

Step 5: Print n and increment n by 1(n=n+1).

Step 5: Repeat the process till the condition n<10 is reached

Step 6: Stop.

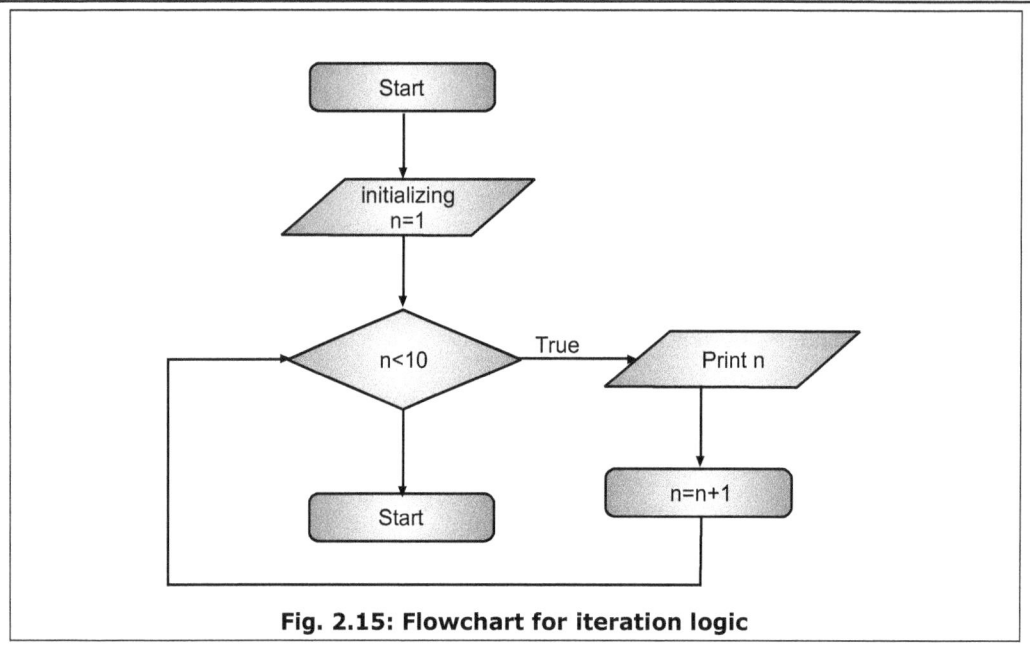

Fig. 2.15: Flowchart for iteration logic

2.10 Functions

A function is a block of code that has a name and it has a property that it is reusable i.e. it can be executed from as many different points in a C Program as requireD) Function groups a number of program statements into a unit and gives it a name. This unit can be invoked from other parts of a program. A computer program cannot handle all the tasks by itself. Instead it requests other program like entities – called functions in C – to get its tasks done. A function is a self contained block of statements that perform a coherent task of same kind

The name of the function is unique in a C Program and is Global. It means that a function can be accessed from any location within a C Program. We pass information to the function called arguments specified when the function is called And the function either returns some value to the point it was called from or returns nothing. We can divide a long C program into small blocks which can perform a certain task.

2.10.1 Structure of a Function

There are two main parts of the function. The function header and the function body.

FPL – I ENGG. (F.E. SEM. I)   INTRODUCTION

```
int sum(int x, int y)
{
        int ans = 0;      //holds the answer that will be returned
        ans = x + y;      //calculate the sum
        return ans        //return the answer
}
```

1. Function Header

In the first line of the above code

`int sum(int x, int y)`

It has three main parts

1. The name of the function i.e. sum
2. The parameters of the function enclosed in parenthesis
3. Return value type i.e. int

2. Function Body

Whatever is written with in { } in the above example is the body of the function.

3. Function Prototypes

The prototype of a function provides the basic information about a function which tells the compiler that the function is used correctly or not. It contains the same information as the function header contains. The prototype of the function in the above example would be like

`int sum (int x, int y);`

The only difference between the header and the prototype is the semicolon ; there must the a semicolon at the end of the prototype.

Multiple Choice Questions

1. A sentinel is also called as a _____.
   - A) Variable
   - B) Counter
   - C) True value
   - D) Flag value

2. Method which uses a list of well-defined instructions to complete a task, starting from a given initial state to end state, is called _____.
   - A) Program
   - B) Algorithm
   - C) High level Language
   - D) Flowchart

3. Flow chart helps for _____ .
   A) Better communication   B) Efficient coding
   C) Program Testing   D) A & B

4. Basic symbols of flow chart are _____ .
   A) Start and End   B) Processing, Decision
   C) Input – Output   D) All of above

5. Diamond shape in flow chart denotes _____ .
   A) Start   B) Decision
   C) End   D) Input - Output task

6. The chart that contains only function flow and no code is called as a _____.
   A) Structure chart   B) Function chart
   C) Flowchart   D) Pseudo chart

7. Which digits is/are used in a binary number system?
   A) 0 and 2   B) 1 and -1
   C) 0 and 1   D) 0 and 1 and 2

8. Which of the following shape is used for representing a Conditional Statement in a Flow chart?
   A) Parallelogram   B) Rhombus
   C) Trapezoid   D) Rectangle

9. Amongst the flowchart symbols, which of the following is an Auxiliary symbol?
   A) Sequence   B) Connector
   C) Decision   D) repetition

10. ROM is the _____ .
    A) volatile memory   B) non-volatile memory
    C) virtual memory   D) none of the above

11. Amongst the following symbols, which of the following is not a symbol used in a flowchart?
    A) Star   B) Terminal Box
    C) Input-Output Box   D) Diamond

12. RAM stands for _____ .
    A) Read only memory   B) Random access memory
    C) Recently Acquired Memory D) Read Ahead Memory

13. Which of the following is not the type of the printer?
    A) dot matrix printer   B) laser printer
    C) drum printer   D) scanner
14. Algorithm and Flowchart help us to_____
    A) Know the memory capacity
    B) Identify the base of a number system
    C) Direct the output to a printer
    D) Specify the problem completely and clearly
15. Which of the following is not the part of the computer?
    A) Monitor   B) Hard disk   C) RAM   D) Printer
16. The operations included in the instruction set of a computer are _____.
    A) Logical   B) Arithmetic   C) Input-Output   D) All of the above
17. In a flowchart, a Data File is represented by a _____ shape.
    A) Diamond   B) Parallelogram   C) Rectangle   D) Cylinder
18. A good algorithm should not _____.
    A) Execute for a given set of initial conditions
    B) Produce the correct output
    C) Terminate after finite number of steps
    D) Result into ambiguous state
19. _____ is used to write the algorithms.
    A) Computer Language C   B) Computer Language C++
    C) Any Programming Language D) English Language
20. Which of the followings is a program planning tool?
    A) Compiler   B) Flow Charts   C) Pseudo Code   D) Both B and C
21. The main memory is also called as the _____.
    A) Primary memory   B) Cache memory
    C) Secondary memory   D) Auxillary Memory
22. Which amongst the following flowchart symbols is a ` two way ` branching symbol?
    A) Parellogram   B) Connecter
    C) Diamond   D) Rectangle

23. Parallelogram is used to represent _____ in a flowchart.
    A) Decision   B) Processing
    C) Termination   D) Input and Output

24. Connector in a flowchart represents _____ .
    A) Arithmetic operation   B) Data movement operation
    C) Comparison operation   D) None of the above

25. Detailed flowchart is also called as _____ .
    A) Macro flowchart   B) Micro flowchart
    C) Mini flowchart   D) None of the above

26. Macro flowchart is also called as _____ .
    A) Less detail flowchart   B) More detail flowchart
    C) Simple flowchart   D) None of the above

27. Sentinel value is used to _____ .
    A) Start a loop   B) Terminate a loop
    C) Input value   D) Output value

28. Goto statement is used for _____ .
    A) Conditional jump only
    B) Unconditional jump only
    C) both conditional and unconditional jumps
    D) None of the above

29. The loop condition is tested at the ----------of the 'do...while' construct.
    A) Start   B) End   C) Middle   D) Start & End

30. There is no symbol for expressing _____ while drawing a flowchart or writing an algorithm.
    A) Assertion   B) Comparison   C) Negation   D) No Action

31. A program design tool in which standard graphical symbols are used to represent the logical flow of data is called as a _____.
    A) Flowchart   B) Pseudo code
    C) Algorithm   D) Structured Chart

32. The difference between main memory and secondary storage is that the main memory is_____ and the secondary storage is _____.
    A) Temporary, permanent   B) Permanent, temporary
    C) Slow, fast   D) None of the above

33. Which of the following is an iterative control structure?
    A) Decision Making   B) Sequential
    C) Jump   D) Loop
34. The data seen on a monitor is called as the _____ of the data
    A) Soft copy   B) Hard copy   C) True copy   D) All of the above
35. Secondary storage is also known as _____.
    A) Primary Memory   B) Ancillary Memory
    C) An Auxiliary Memory   D) Read Only Memory
36. Which of the following structures are used in computer programs
    A) Sequential B) Decision   C) Iterative   D) All of above
37. Which of the following scenario is correct?
    A) flowchart->algorithm->programming language
    B) flowchart->programming language->algorithm
    C) algorithm->flow chart->programming language
    D) algorithm->programming language->flow chart
38. Instructions in algorithms should be _____ .
    A) Precise   B) Unambiguous
    C) Precise & Unambiguous D) None of above
39. The instructions in machine language must be in streams of _____ .
    A) decimal digits   B) ASCII code   C) 0s and 1s   D) UNICODE
40. The central computer, which may be a powerful microcomputer, minicomputer or mainframe in a computer network is known as the _____ .
    A) Terminal   B) Client   C) Server   D) Node
41. The printed copy of the data is also called as the _____ .
    A) Softcopy   B) Hardcopy
    C) True copy   D) None of the above
42. Which of the following statement does not belong to structured programming?
    A) While   B) Do-while   C) For   D) goto
43. As compared to a flowchart, it is easier to modify the _____ of a program logic when program modifications are necessary.
    A) Macro flowchart   B) Micro flowchart
    C) Terminal   D) Pseudo code

44. Algorithm halts in _____
    A) Finite time   B) Infinite time
    C) Logarithmic time   D) Exponential time
45. What does IBM stands for?
    A) Indian Business machine   B) International Business Machine
    C) Indian Business Model   D) International Business Model
46. Today's computers belong to _____ generation.
    A) Third   B) Fifth   C) Fourth   D) Second
47. CD-ROM is a_____.
    A) Semiconductor memory   B) Optical memory
    C) Magnetic memory   D) None of the above
48. A digital system uses _____ number system.
    A) Binary   B) Decimal   C) Octal   D) Hexadecimal
49. Base of hexadecimal number system is.
    A) 2   B) 8   C) 10   D) 16
50. In which discipline s), an algorithm is used _____?
    A) Mathematics   B) Computing
    C) Linguistics   D) All of above
51. How many nibbles a byte contains?
    A) 2   B) 8   C) 4   D) 6
52. The _____ flow chart symbols represents one way flow of control.
    A) Processing   B) Decision   C) Terminal   D) All above
53. What is an infinite loop?
    A) It is an endless loop   B) It means multiple loops
    C) It is a nested loop   D) It is an unclosed loop
54. The 2 s complement of 1000 is
    A) 111   B) 101   C) 1000   D) 1
55. The condition is tested at the -----------of loop in a 'while' statement
    A) Start   B) End   C) Middle   D) Any Where
56. The normal flow of flowchart is from _____ .
    A) Left to Right   B) Right to Left
    C) A & D   D) Top to Bottom

57. The arithmetic operations are carried out using _____.
    A) Output Device   B) ALU
    C) Memory Device   D) Timing & Control Unit
58. Variables are named area of _____ that is used to hold data
    A) memory locations
    B) row and column number on a monitor
    C) row and column number on a printer
    D) none of the above
59. Base of octal number system is.
    A) 2   B) 8   C) 10   D) 16
60. Which of the following are characteristics of a good programming language?
    A) Safety   B) Simplicity   C) Performance   D) All of the above
61. Which tool shows textual design solution?
    A) Flowchart   B) Structure chart
    C) Pseudo code   D) Algorithm
62. Which is the smallest unit of memory?
    A) Byte   B) Nibble   C) Bit   D) Word
63. Finiteness property of an Algorithm is _____
    A) The number of steps in the algorithm should be finite.
    B) The algorithm should terminate after a finite no. of times .
    C) For all possible combinations of input data, the algorithm terminates after a finite no. of steps.
    D) None of above
64. Terminal symbol in a flow chart indicates _____ .
    A) Decision   B) End
    C) Process   D) None of the above
65. A set of registers is one part of_____.
    A) Input device   B) Control unit
    C) Output device   D) Central Processing Unit
66. Execution of two or more programs by a single CPU is known as_____.
    A) Multiprocessing   B) Time sharing
    C) Multiprogramming   D) None of the above

67. Laptops are also known as _____ Computers
    A) Mainframe   B) Super
    C) Notebook   D) Personal
68. _____ statement is used to indicate the end of a 'DO..WHILE' construct in the pseudo code
    A) END DO   B) DO END   C) END   D) CLOSE
69. The binary number system uses base of
    A) 2   B) 8   C) 10   D) 16
70. How many bits a byte contains ?
    A) 2   B) 8   C) 4   D) 6
71. Which of the following is not a program planning tool ?
    A) Flowchart   B) Structure chart   C) Pseudo codes   D) Loop
72. In which of the following scenario, sequence logic will not be used?
    A) Accepting an input from the user.
    B) Comparing two sets of data
    C) Giving an output to the user.
    D) Adding two numbers
73. Common sentinel values use a ` Null ` character for indicating
    A) The end of a null-terminated string.
    B) The last string.
    C) The previous of last string.
    D) None of above
74. If we want to choose between one of the two tasks then, _____ structure is used
    A) IF...THEN...ELSE   B) FOR
    C) REPEAT-UNTIL   D) DO WHILE
75. Actual execution of instructions in a computer takes place in
    A) ALU   B) Control Unit
    C) Storage unit   D) None of the above
76. The use of mathematical logic for computer programming is also called _____ .
    A) Physical Programming   B) Logical Programming
    C) View Programming   D) Computer Programming

77. Information retrieval is faster from _____
    A) Floppy disk   B) Magnetic tape
    C) Hard disk   D) None of the above

78. A good algorithm is not _____
    A) Simple and powerful
    B) Clear for implementation
    C) Dependent on a particular machine
    D) effective

79. The basic operations performed by a computer are _____
    A) Arithmetic operation   B) Logical operation
    C) Input and Output   D) All the above

80. Pseudo code instructions are phrases written in a _____.
    A) machine language   B) assembly language
    C) high level language   D) natural language

81. A Pixel is _____
    A) A computer program that draws picture
    B) A picture stored in secondary memory
    C) The smallest part of a picture
    D) None of these

82. The _____ is a program design tool that is a visual representation of the logic in a program.
    A) Flow chart   B) Structure chart
    C) Program Map   D) Waterfall model

83. Which device is used commonly as the standard pointing device in a Graphical User Environment
    A) Keyboard   B) Mouse   C) Joystick   D) Track ball

84. Which of the following is an input device?
    A) Monitor   B) Mouse   C) Printer   D) Editor

85. Which of the following is an output device?
    A) Monitor   B) Keyboard   C) Touch-screen   D) Mouse

86. English statements that follow a loosely defined syntax & are used to convey the design of an algorithm is called _____.
    A) Program   B) Flowchart
    C) Pseudo code   D) None of the above.

87. Which technology is used in reading a Compact disk?
    A) Mechanical B) Electrical
    C) Electro Magnetic D) Optical

88. Which of the following have the fastest access time?
    A) Semiconductor Memories B) Magnetic Disks
    C) Magnetic Tapes D) Compact Disks

89. A flowchart is used in _____ of the software development.
    A) Implementation phase B) Testing phase
    C) Analysis phase D) Design phase

90. Which of the following is the smallest and fastest computer?
    A) Super computer B) Quantum computer
    C) Micro Computer D) Mini Computer

91. Any program can be written using _____ .
    A) Selection logic
    B) Sequence and selection logic
    C) Iterative logic
    D) Sequence, selection and Iterative logic

92. Writing a code is a part of _____ in software development life cycle.
    A) Implementation phase B) Testing phase
    C) Analysis phase D) Design phase

93. Indentation is used to format _____ .
    A) Program source code B) Object code
    C) Executable code D) All of the above

94. Selection logic is known as _____ .
    A) Decision logic B) Sequence Logic
    C) Iteration logic D) All of the above

95. Another name for pseudo code is _____ .
    A) Imitation code B) Flowchart
    C) Program D) Algorithm

96. In do-while loop, loop condition is checked at the _____ .
    A) Beginning of loop B) End of loop
    C) End of program D) Start of program

97. How many basic symbols are available to draw a flowchart?
    A) 4	B) 6	C) 8	D) 7
98. Which of the following is not the way to represent an algorithm?
    A) As an executable code	B) As a program
    C) As a flowchart	D) As a pseudo code
99. Consider the following statements and determine which of the following is correct?
    a) Indentation makes programs more readable and simpler to understand
    b) Indentation is compulsory while writing a program
    A) Only a) is true	B) Only b) is true
    C) Both a) and b) are true	D) Both a) and b) are false
100. Which of the following statement is false?
    A) Flowchart provides graphical representation of program logic
    B) Drawing a flowchart before writing the program is better
    C) Pseudo code gives graphical representation of program logic
    D) Writing pseudo code before writing the program is better
101. Which of the following statements is correct?
    A) Flowchart is a pictorial representation of an algorithm
    B) Pseudo code is an analysis tool used for planning program logic
    C) Both A and B are false
    D) Both A and B are true
102. A structured chart is _____
    A) A statement of information processing requirements
    B) A hierarchical partitioning of the program
    C) A document of what has to be accomplished
    D) All of the above
103. Connector in flowchart is represented by _____
    A) Rectangle	B) Diamond	C) ellipse	D) Circle
104. A rectangle in flowchart denotes _____
    A) Start of Program
    B) Input or output function
    C) Arithmetic and data movement instruction
    D) End of Program

105. In a flowchart, flow lines are used to indicate _____
    A) Beginning of program B) Data movement
    C) Flow of operations D) All of the above
106. Which of the following symbol is not used while drawing flowchart?
    A) Terminal B) Input/output
    C) Processing D) Control
107. Infinite loops can be avoided by using _____
    A) Sentinel B) Counter C) Algorithm D) Both A & B
108. The valid symbols in flowchart is/are _____
    A) Connector B) Terminal Symbol
    C) Processing Symbol D) All of above
109. Structure charts are read in _____ direction.
    A) left-right, top-down B) top-down, left-right
    C) down-up, left-right D) top-down, right-left
110. Functional flow of a program is shown by _____
    A) Flowchart B) Pseudo code
    C) Structure chart D) Program Map
111. The series of interrelated phases that is used to develop computer software is known as _____
    A) Program development B) System development life cycle
    C) System Analysis D) System Design
112. An algorithm is represented as _____ .
    A) Program B) Flow charts C) Pseudo Codes D) All of above
113. A diamond is used in flowcharts to represent _____ .
    A) Arithmetic & data movement instructions
    B) Input
    C) Output
    D) Decision
114. The _____ is a program design tool that visually represents the solution logic
    A) Flowchart B) Program map
    C) Pseudo code D) Structure chart

115. The term algorithm refers to _____
    A) step by step description of how to arrive at the solution of problem.
    B) it is a kind of flow chart.
    C) it is a set of instructions in specified sequence.
    D) All of the above.

116. Pseudo code is used to _____
    A) Run a program
    B) Compile a program
    C) Plan program logic using natural language
    D) Debug a program

117. Any program can be written using _____ structures.
    A) Sequence logic, Merge logic, Insertion logic
    B) Sequence logic, Selection logic, Iteration logic
    C) Sequence logic, Branch logic, Iteration logic
    D) None of the above

118. Algorithm can be represented in following ways except
    A) as a program
    B) as a flowchart
    C) as a process
    D) as a pseudo code

119. Rectangle can be used for representing _____
    A) decision
    B) processing
    C) input-output
    D) none of these

120. Which one of the following is the disadvantage of a flowchart?
    A) Efficient coding
    B) Systematic Debugging
    C) Better Communication
    D) None of these

121. The algorithm cannot be represented as _____
    A) a flowchart
    B) a program
    C) a process
    D) a pseudocode

122. Iteration logic is used to execute instructions _____
    A) Depending upon some condition to choose one of the path
    B) One after another
    C) Several times depending upon some condition
    D) None of the above

123. Decision symbol can be used for _____
    A) A two way branch decision   B) A three way branch decision
    C) Multiple way branch decision D) All of the above
124. DO...WHILE and REPEAT....UNTIL structure are called _____
    A) Sequential logic structures   B) Decision logic structures
    C) Iterative logic structures   D) None of the above
125. IF...THEN...ELSE or CASE structure are called _____
    A) Selection logic structures   B) Sequence logic structures
    C) Iteration logic structures   D) Program logic structures
126. Loops in a program are written using _____
    A) Selection logic   B) Iteration logic
    C) Sequence logic   D) None of the above
127. Which out of the following is not a type of operation performed by a computer?
    A) Arithmetic B) Logical C) Emotional D) Mathematical
128. Result of logical operation is _____ .
    A) Boolean B) Integer C) Character D) String
129. Which of the following logic is used to produce loops in progarmme logic?
    A) sequence logic   B) selection logic
    C) iteration logic   D) none of them
130. Flow lines are used for _____ .
    A) connecting from one page to another page
    B) input-output
    C) Decision logic
    D) Indicate flow of program
131. What is the first phase of Program Development Life Cycle?
    A) Design B) Testing C) Coding D) Analysis
132. Each step in an algorithm should be performed in a _____ time.
    A) Finite B) Infinite C) short D) Long
133. Where does a computer adds and compares data?
    A) Floppy Disk   B) CD Rom
    C) ALU   D) Hard Disk

Unit 2 | 2.36

134. What is PDLC?
    A) Product development life cycle   B) Plan development life cycle
    C) Project development life cycle   D) Program development life cycle
135. Which of the following is not used as a logic structure while writing ` C ` programs?
    A) sequence logic   B) process logic
    C) selection logic   D) iteration logic
136. A computer program consists of the _____ .
    A) a flowchart
    B) an algorithm
    C) algorithm written using some programming language
    D) both an algorithm and a flowchart
137. What is the result of design phase in PDLC?
    A) Algorithm & flowchart   B) Program
    C) Algorithm only   D) Flowchart only
138. The default flow of control, particularly in imperative programming is _____
    A) Parallel   B) Sequential
    C) Random   D) None of the above
139. The most important aspect of program coding is _____
    A) Readability   B) Usability
    C) Productivity   D) All of the above
140. Which of the following is not a characteristic of a good programming language?
    A) Simplicity   B) Naturalness   C) Locality   D) Complexity
141. Which of the following statement is not appropriate?
    A) Indentation improves the performance of the program.
    B) Indentation is needed to make the program more readable.
    C) Indentation helps the program to distinguish control statements.
    D) Indentation makes the program easy to debug.
142. In flowcharts, ellipse is used for denoting _____ .
    A) Start only   B) Stop only
    C) Both Start and End   D) None of these

143. The _____ symbol is used to indicate the beginning, ending, and pauses in the program logic flow.
    A) Flow lines
    B) Processing
    C) Input/output
    D) Terminal.

144. Arithmetic operations are _____ type of operation.
    A) Input
    B) Output
    C) Processing
    D) Decision Making

145. Program planning enables a programmer to _____ .
    A) write program instruction in correct sequence
    B) ensure that program instructions are appropriate for the problem
    C) Both A and B are True
    D) None of these

146. Which of the following statement cannot change the flow direction of program?
    A) Function Call
    B) Null statement
    C) for statement
    D) goto statement

147. To write the correct and effective program we must first _____
    A) Draw a flowchart
    B) Plan its logic
    C) Write the pseudo code
    D) All of the above

148. Pseudo code is also called as the_____.
    A) Program Design Language (PDL)
    B) Micro flowchart
    C) Imitation
    D) Decision

149. The sentinel value used should be _____ .
    A) always zero
    B) always negative integer
    C) always positive integer
    D) value which don t occur in that block

150. In structure charts modules are described as _____ .
    A) circle   B) triangle   C) rectangle   D) ellipse

151. Software design plays important role in?
    A) Developing software
    B) Delivering software
    C) Denying software
    D) All of above

FPL – I ENGG. (F.E. SEM. I)   INTRODUCTION

152. What are Hungarian notations?
    A) Writing loops   B) Manipulating pointers
    C) To write variable name   D) Flowchart notations

153. Pseudo code emphasize on the _____ aspect of a program.
    A) Development   B) Coding
    C) design   D) debugging

154. The similarity between structure charts and flow charts is _____ .
    A) both of them use top-down approach
    B) both of them use bottom-up approach
    C) both of them provide pictorial view
    D) none of them hide specific language syntax

155. In which of the following scenario, the sequence logic will not be used?
    A) Accepting an input from the user.
    B) Comparing two sets of data
    C) Giving an output to the user.
    D) Adding two numbers.

Answers

1.	D	2.	B	3.	D	4.	D	5.	B
6.	B	7.	C	8.	B	9.	B	10.	B
11.	A	12.	B	13.	D	14.	D	15.	D
16.	D	17.	D	18.	D	19.	D	20.	D
21.	A	22.	C	23.	D	24.	D	25.	B
26.	A	27.	B	28.	B	29.	B	30.	D
31.	A	32.	A	33.	D	34.	A	35.	C
36.	D	37.	A	38.	C	39.	C	40.	C
41.	B	42.	D	43.	D	44.	A	45.	B
46.	B	47.	B	48.	A	49.	D	50.	B
51.	A	52.	A	53.	A	54.	C	55.	B
56.	D	57.	B	58.	A	59.	B	60.	D
61.	C	62.	C	63.	C	64.	B	65.	D

66.	C	67.	C	68.	A	69.	A	70.	B
71.	D	72.	B	73.	A	74.	A	75.	A
76.	B	77.	C	78.	C	79.	D	80.	D
81.	C	82.	A	83.	B	84.	B	85.	A
86.	C	87.	D	88.	A	89.	D	90.	B
91.	D	92.	A	93.	A	94.	A	95.	A
96.	B	97.	B	98.	A	99.	A	100.	C
101.	D	102.	B	103.	D	104.	C	105.	C
106.	D	107.	D	108.	D	109.	B	110.	C
111.	B	112.	D	113.	D	114.	A	115.	A
116.	C	117.	B	118.	C	119.	B	120.	D
121.	C	122.	C	123.	D	124.	C	125.	A
126.	B	127.	C	128.	A	129.	C	130.	D
131.	D	132.	A	133.	C	134.	D	135.	B
136.	C	137.	A	138.	B	139.	D	140.	C
141.	A	142.	C	143.	D	144.	C	145.	C
146.	B	147.	D	148.	A	149.	D	150.	C
151.	A	152.	C	153.	C	154.	C	155.	A

C PROGRAMMING

Syllabus

Character set, Constant, Variables, Keywords and Comments; Operator and Operator Precedence. Statements. I/O Operations; Preprocessor Directives. Pointers, Arrays and Strings. User Define Data Types – Structure and Union.

3.1 Introduction to Programming languages

Computers were developed to perform the all arithmetic and logical operations accurately and in time efficient manner. As computer is an electronic machine so it can understand only language of zero and one, which is also called as binary language. The 0 in binary language represents the absence of power supply whereas 1 represents the presence of power supply.

In early days of computers, to perform arithmetic and logical operations programs were written in terms of 0 and 1. But it was very difficult to understand the language of 0's and 1's. So Alan Turing wrote the set of shorthand codes to speed up and ease the computer programming. After which the notion of programming language was introduced which includes the set of characters with specified rules.

FORTRAN is the First high level programming language, which was developed by John Backus at IBM in year 1954 and released commercially in year 1957. FORTRAN is an acronym for Formula Translation, because it was developed to translate mathematical formulas into computer code. The algorithm language which is also called as ALGOL was developed in year 1958. In year 1972, C language was derived from ALGOL language.

3.2 Introduction to C languages

Dennis Ritchie at bell laboratory developed C language in year 1972. Most of the features of C language were derived from B language. Due to flexibility of C language UNIX operating system which was initially written in assembly language was again rewritten in C language.

- C language is a structure oriented programming language.
- C language is a procedure-oriented language.
- In C language complete program is composed of various functions and procedures.
- C language follows Top-Down approach in program design.
- In 1978, Dennis Ritchie and Brian Kernighan published the first edition "The C Programming Language" and commonly known as K&R C.
- In 1983, the American National Standards Institute (ANSI) established a committee to provide a modern, comprehensive definition of C. The resulting definition, the ANSI standard, or "ANSI C", was completed in late 1988.

Features of C language

- **Reliability:** C language allows low-level access to data and commands and maintains the syntax of a high-level language. These qualities make it a useful language for both systems programming and general purpose programs.
- **Flexibility:** C is a powerful and flexible language, which provides fast program execution.
- **Modularity:** The codes of C language can be stored in libraries so that programmer can reuse it.
- **Efficiency and Effectiveness:** The programs of C language are less complex and do not require any special programming language platform other than compiler. C language plays vital role in hardware programming.

Introduction to C Programming

C language is the case sensitive language. To execute the program of C language user required Turbo C compiler. User has to save C program with the extension .C.

Following are the basic commands, which form the basic part of every C program.

Sr. No.	Command	Explanation
1.	#include<stdio.h>	This is a preprocessor command that includes standard input output header file(stdio.h) from the C library before compiling a C program
2.	#include<conio.h>	This is a preprocessor command that includes console input output header file(conio.h) from the C library before compiling a C program
3.	main()	This is the main function from where execution of any C program begins
4.	/* some comments */	/* --- */ is used to comment the block of instructions. The instructions inside /* -- */ won't be considered by C compiler
5.	printf(" ----");	printf is the output function used to print the output onto the screen.
6.	scanf(" ----");	Scanf is the input function used to take input from the user.
7.	clrscr();	This function is used to to clear the output of previous program from the screen.
8.	getch();	This function is used to hold the output screen

Compile and execute C program:

- Compilation is the process of converting a C program from user readable code to machine level code.
- Compiler is responsible to find out all the syntactic and semantic error from the program.
- Alt+F9 key is used to compile the C program.
- This compilation process is done by a compiler which is an inbuilt program in C.
- After the successful compilation, C program is converted into another file called executable file. This is also called as binary file.
- User can execute the binary file with the help of (Ctrl+F9) key.

Sample C program to print Hello word

```c
#include <stdio.h>
#include <conio.h>
void main( )
{
clrscr( );
printf("\n Hello World!");
getch( );
}
```

Output

Hello World!

Description

This program prints hello world.

- The first two lines in the programs begin with symbol # which is also known as preprocessor. Preprocessor is responsible to perform specific task before the actual compilation of programs begins.
- In first two instructions preprocessor is responsible to include header file 'stdio.h'. This is the standard input output header file which contains the definition of all input and output functions like printf and scanf. In second instruction, preprocessor is responsible to include header file conio.h. Header file conio.h contains the definitions of all functions related to console like clrscr and getch.
- Third line of the program is void main(). Compilation of every C program starts with the main function. Void is the return type of 'main' function which indicated that main function is not returning any value.
- The curly brackets {} are used to define the scope of main function.
- The fifth line of the program contains the 'clrscr' function which is responsible to provide blank output screen to the user by deleting all the outputs of previous programs.
- The sixth line of the program contains the 'printf' function which is responsible to print output on the screen. The text written inside the two double quotes is printed on the output screen other than escape sequences. In the above

program \n is the escape sequence which is used print output on the next line.
- The seventh line of the program contains the getch function which is acronym for get character. The function getch is responsible to hold the output screen till user enters extra key from the keyboard.

Example 2 - C program to take input from user using 'scanf' function

```
#include <stdio.h>
#include <conio.h>
void main( )
{
int number;
clrscr( );
printf("Enter an integer\n");
scanf("%d",&number);
printf("number entered by you is %d\n",
getch( );
}
```

Output

Enter a number

5

number entered by you is 5

Description

The above program is same as that of previous program instead of line number five and eight.
- In the fifth line of the program programmer declare variable 'number'. The datatype 'int' is indicated that the variable number is of type integer. Datatype is also responsible to allocate memory to the variables.
- The eighth line of the program contains the 'scanf' function which is responsible to take input from the user. The '%d' inside scanf function indicates that the value entered by the user is considered as an integer value and '&number' indicates that the value entered by used is saved at the address of variable 'number'.

3.3 Character Set

The character set of C language is categorized into two types

1. **Graphic characters:** Graphic characters are the set of characters which are as it is printed on the output screen. Graphic character set of C language contains al types of letters, digits and special symbols which are used to represent information.

   A) **Letters:** Letters in graphical character set contains all the letters from a – z. As C is case sensitive language, letters from a – z have different meaning than letters from A – Z.

   B) **Digits:** Graphical character set contains the digits from 0 -9.

   C) **Special Symbol:** Special symbol in graphical character set contains following symbol to represent an information.

Symbol	Meaning
~	Tilde
!	Exclamation mark
#	Number sign or hash
$	Dollar sign
%	Percent sign
^	Caret
&	Ampersand
*	Asterisk
(	Left parenthesis
)	Right parenthesis
_	Underscore
+	Plus sign
|	Vertical bar
\	Backslash
`	Apostrophe
-	Minus sign
=	Equal to sign
{	Left brace

	}	Right brace
	[	Left bracket
	]	Right bracket
	:	Colon
	"	Quotation mark
	;	Semicolon
	<	Opening angle bracket
	>	Closing angle bracket
	?	Question mark
	,	Comma
	.	Period
	/	Slash OR Forward slash

2. Non-graphic characters: Non-graphical character set contains characters which are not printed as it is on output screen but responsible for the formatting of text in terms of length and dimensions. Non-graphical character set contains all types of escape sequences. Following are the examples of escape sequences.

Character	Meaning	Character	Meaning
\a	Audible alert(bell)	\v	Vertical tab
\n	New line	\f	Form Carriage return
\r	Carriage return	\t	Horizontal tab
\b	Back space		

3.4 Constants

These are the quantities whose value is not going to change throughout the program. Keyword const is used to declare the quantity as a constant. Constants can be a character, digit or set of characters. Once the constant is declare user is not allow to modify its value. Constant can be of integer type, floating type, character or string type value. Syntax for declaring constants are as follows

int const a = 1;

3.5 Variables

Variables are the quantities whose values can be changed during the execution of program. Variables are used to hold the values of other data members. Memory is allocated at the time of declaration of variable. Size of memory depends on the data type of variable. Syntax for defining variable is as follows

       Data type   variable name;

Data types : Data types are used to indicate the type of variable. Data types are also responsible to allocate memory to the variable. There are four basic data types available in C. Each data type has its own size and range which is also depends on the size of operating system. Following Specification of data types are according to 32 bit operating system.

Data type	Description	Memory consumed	Ranges of values
int	Holds Non-fractional Integer Value	2 bytes	-32768 to $+32767$
char	Holds Single character	1 byte	-128 to 127
float	Holds fractional Integer Value	4 bytes	$3.4\ e^{-38}$ to $3.4\ e^{+38}$
Double	Holds big fractional Integer Value (double)	8 bytes	$1.7\ e^{-308}$ to $1.7\ e^{+308}$

Modifiers/Qualifiers: Modifiers/Qualifiers are used to categorize the data type and also define the amount of storage allocated to the variable. There are four basic modifiers short, long, signed and unsigned.

TYPE	SIZE (Bytes)	Range	Format
Signed int or Int	2	-32768 to 32767	%d
Unsigned int	2	0 to 65535	%u
Short int or Signed short int	1	-128 to 127	%d
Unsigned short int	1	0 to 255	%u
Long int or signed long int	4	-2147483648 to 2147483647	%ld
Unsigned long int	4	0 to 4294967295	%lu
Char or Signed Char	1	-128 to 127	%c
Unsigned Char	1	0 to 255	%c
Float	4	$3.4\ e-38$ to $3.4\ e+38$	%f
Double	8	$1.7e-308$ to $1.7e+308$	%lf
Long Double	10	$3.4\ e-4932$ to $3.4\ e+4932$	%lf

Variable Name: Variable Name may contain of letters, digits and one special symbol (_) with following rules.
- The first character in the variable name must be a letter.
- Commas or blank spaces are not allowed within a variable name.
- There should not be any special symbol other than an underscore (_) can be used in a variable name.

Example: int a;

Here 'a' is the name of variable and it is of type of type integer so total memory allocated for variable 'a' is 2 bytes.

There are two types of variable

1. **Local Variable:** Local variable are only accessible in the block of code in which they are declare. The scopes of local variables are limited to the function in which they are declared.

2. **Global Variable:** Global variable are accessible throughout the program after their declaration.

3.6 Keywords

Keywords are the special words which have its pre-define meaning in C language. All the Keywords in C language are written in lowercase. Keyword cannot be used as a variable name in C language. There are total 32 keywords in C language, which are listed below

auto	double	int	struct
break	else	long	switch
case	enum	register	typedef
char	extern	return	union
const	float	short	unsigned
continue	for	signed	while
default	goto	sizeof	void
do	if	static	volatile

Comments: Comments are the non executable part of program. Comments are used for the documentation purpose. C language provide two syntax for comments

1. Single line comment: Two forward slash (//) are useful in making the single line as a comment. Compiler will not consider the instruction written after the Two forward slash.

2. Block of Comment: To make block of instructions as a comment, C language provide (/* instructions */) syntax. Compiler will not consider the instructions written inside the two stars.

3.7 Operator and Operator Precedence

Every expression in C language contains set of operators and operands. Operators are the special symbols which are used to indicate the type of operation whereas operands are the data member or variables operating as per operation specified by operator. One expression contains one or more set of operators and operands. So to avoid the ambiguity in execution of expression, C compiler fixed the precedence of operator. Depending on the operation, operators are classified into following category.

1. Arithmetic Operator: These are the operator which are useful in performing mathematical calculations. Following are the list of arithmetic operator in C language. To understand the operation assume variable A contains value 10 and variable contains value 5.

Sr. No.	Operator	Discription	Example
1.	+	Used to add two operands	Result of A+B is 15
2.	-	Used to subtract two operands	Result of A-B is 5
3.	*	Used to multiply two operands	Result of A*B is 50
4.	/	Used to divide two operands	Result of A/B is 2
5.	%	Find reminder of the division of two operand	Result of A%B is 0

2. Relational Operators: Relational operator are used to compare two operands. Relational operator produce result in terms of binary values. It returns 1 when the result is true and 0 when result is false. Following are the list of relational operator in C language. To understand the operation assume variable 'A' contains value 10 and variable 'B' contains value 5.

Sr. No.	Operator	Discription	Example
1.	<	This is 'less than' operator which is used to check whether the value of left operand is less than the value of right operand or not	Result of A<B is false
2.	>	This is 'greater than' operator which is used to check whether the value of left operand is greater than the value of right operand or not	Result of A>B is true
3.	<=	This is 'less than or equal to' operator	Result of A<=B is false
4.	>=	This is 'greater than or equal to' operator	Result of A>=B is true
5.	==	This is equal to operator which is used to check value of both operansds are equal or not	Result of A==B is false
6.	!=	This is 'not equal to' operator which is used to check value of both operansds are equal or not	Result of A!=B is true

3. Logical Operators: Logical operators are used to compare logical values of two operands. Following are the list of logical operator in C language. To understand the operation assume variable A contains value 10 and variable contains value 5.

Sr. No.	Operator	Discription	Example
1.	&&	This is logical AND, it returns true when both the values are non zero	Result of (A&&B) is true
2.	||	This is logical OR, it returns true when any of two value is non zero	Result of (A||B) is true
3.	!	This is logical NOT operator, it is used to reverse the logical state of operand	Result of !(A&&B) is false

4. Assignment Operators: Assignment operator is used to assign the value to variable. To understand the operation assume variable A contains value 10 and variable 'B' contains value 5.

Example: A=B;

in the above example value of variable B is assign to variable A. Result of this expression is value of A is 5 and value of B is 5.

5. Increments and Decrement Operators: These operator are used to increase or decrease the value of variable by one. To understand the operation assume variable 'A' contains value 10.

Sr. No.	Operator	Discription	Example
1.	++	This is incremental operator which is used to increase the value of variable by 1	Result of (A++) is value of A is 11
2.	--	This is decremental operator which is used to decrease the value of variable by 1	Result of (A--) is value of A is 9

6. **Bitwise Operators:** These operators are used to work on the each bits of data. These operators can work on the binary data. If the data is non binary then computer first of all convert it into binary form and then perform the operation. Following are the list of logical operator in C language. To understand the operation assume variable 'A' contains value 10 and 'B' variable contains value 5. So the binary values of

A = 0000 1010 and

B = 0000 0101

Sr. No.	Operator	Discription	Example
1.	&	This is bitwise AND	Result of (A&B) is 0000 0000 = 0
2.	|	This is bitwise OR	Result of (A|B) is 0000 1111 = 15
3.	^	This is bitwise Exclusive	Result of (A^B) is 0000 1111 = 15
4.	<<	This is used to shift bit on left side	Result of A<<B is 101001010 - 320
5.	>>	This is used to shift bit on right side	Result of A>>B is 0000 0000 = 0

3.8 Statements

Statements in C language consist of tokens, expressions, and set of other statements. Set of statements can be enclosed in the body of one statement. Each statement has its own features and particular syntax. Statements can be classified in to two categories

1. **Branching Statements:** Branching statements are used to select one option among the several other options. Following are the examples of branching statements.(Note: The details of both statements are given in forth unit)

    a) **If Statement:** This statement is used to select one option among two options when the particular condition is satisfied.

b) Switch Statements: This statement is used to select one option by analyzing several other conditions.

2. Looping Statements: looping statements are used to repeat the certain block of code until a particular condition is satisfied. There are three looping statements namely 'while' loop, 'for' loop, 'do-while' loop

(Note: The details of all three looping statements are given in forth unit).

3.9 Input/Output (I/O) Operations

C language provides dedicated functions for the input and output operations. The definitions of both the functions are available in standard input/output header file (stdio.h).

Input Function: Input of program means the feeding data during the execution. Data can feed interms of file and also from the command line. Following are the built in functions which are responsible to take input from the user

1. scanf(): This function is responsible to read data according to the format specified in function and store the input data into the address of specified variable. Syntax of this function is scanf ("format", &var);

2. gets(): This function is responsible to read a string of text from the keyboard and stored in the variable string. Syntax of this function is gets(string);

3. getchar(): This function is responsible to read a single character from the keyboard and stored in the char variable.
Syntax of this function is [ch =]getchar();

Output Function: Output of program means the displaying data after the execution of program. Output can displayed on printer or on the command line screen. Following are the built in functions which are responsible to display output to the user.

1. printf(): This function is responsible to collect data of the variable and display data according to the format specified in function.
Syntax of this function is printf ("format", var);

2. puts(): This function is responsible to display a string of text on the output device.
Syntax of this function is puts (string);

3. putchar(): This function is responsible to display a single character on the output device.
Syntax of this function is putchar (ch);

3.10 Preprocessor Directives

Preprocessor Directives are used to control the preprocessor. Preprocessor directives always start with special symbol hash (#). Because of preprocessor programs are easy to develop, read and modify. Following are the list of preprocessor directives.

Sr. No.	Commands	Discription
1.	#define	use to define constants or any macro substitution
2.	#include	use to includes a file into code.
3.	#if --	use to evaluates a constant integer expression.
4.	#endif	use to terminates conditional text

3.11 Pointers

Pointer is very powerful and useful feature of C programming language. When a variable is declared, there are two things, which are associated with the variable, first is variable value and another one is variables address. Value of a variable can be accesd with the help of variable name but to access the address of the variable we need to take the help of pointers.

Pointers are used to store the address of the variable. Pointers are known as point to variable. Syntax for defining pointer is

> Data Type*pointername

Data type is used to define the type of pointer value then special symbol * followed by pointer name. All the rules of defining name of variable are also applicable while defining name of pointer.

Example:

Sr. No.	Instruction	Description
1.	#include<stdio.h>	Header file included
2.	#include<conio.h>	Header file included
3.	void main()	Execution of program begins

4.	{	Memory is allocated for variable a, b and pointer p
5.	int a=5,b=8,*p;	
6.	clrscr();	Clear the output of previous screen
7.	printf("welcome");	Print "welcome"
8.	printf("\n %d",&a);	Address of variable a is printed
9.	p=&a;	Address of variable a is assign to p
10.	printf("\n %d",p);	Value of p is printed
11.	printf("\n %d",*p);	Value stored at the address of p is printed
12.	printf("\n %d",&p);	Address of pointer p is printed
13.	b=*p;	value stored at address of p is assign to b
14.	printf("\n %d",b);	Value of b is printed on output screen
15.	getch();	Used to hold the output screen
16.	}	Indicates end of scope of main function

3.12 Arrays

Array is a data structure which stores the collection of similar types of element in consecutive memory locations. Indexing of array always start with '0' where as non-graphical variable '\0' indicates the end of array. Syntax for declaring array is

data typearray name[Maximum size];

- Data types are used to define type of element in an array. Data types are also useful in finding the size of total memory locations allocated for the array.
- All the rules of defining name of variable are also applicable for the array name.
- Maximum size indicates the total number of maximum elements that array can hold.
- Total memory allocated for the array is equal to the memory required to store one element of the array multiply by the total element in the array.
- In array memory allocation is done at the time of declaration of an array.

Example:

Sr. No.	Instruction	Description
1.	#include<stdio.h>	Header file included
2.	#include<conio.h>	Header file included
3.	void main()	Execution of program begins
4.	{	Memory is allocated for variable I,n and array a
5.	int i,n,a[10];	
6.	clrscr();	Clear the output of previous screen
7.	printf("enter a number");	Print "enter a number"
8.	scanf("%d",&n);	Input value is stored at the addres of variable n
9.	for(i=0;i<=10;i++)	For loop started from value of i=0 to i=10
10.	{	Compound statement(scope of for loop starts)
11.	a[i]=n*i;	Result of multiplication of n and I is stored at the ith location of array ieas i=0 so it is stores at first location.
12.	printf("\n %d",a[i]);	Value of ith location of the array is printed
13.	}	Compound statement(scope of for loop ends)
14.	printf("\n first element in array is %d",a[0]);	Value of first element of the array is printed
15.	printf("\n fifth element in array is %d",a[4]);	Value of fifth element of the array is printed
16.	printf("\n tenth element in array is %d",a[9]);	Value of tenth element of the array is printed
17.	getch();	Used to hold the output screen
18.	}	Indicates end of scope of main function

3.13 Strings

- Strings are also called as the array of character.
- A special character usually known as null character (\0) is used to indicate the end of the string.

- To read and write the string in C program %s access specifier is required.
- C language provides several built in functions for the manipulation of the string
- To use the built in functions for string, user need to include *string.h* header file.
- Syntax for declaring string is

  char string name[size of string];

char is the data type, user can give any name to the string by following all the rules of defining name of variable. Size of the string is the number of alphabets that user wants to store in string.

Example:

Sr. No.	Instruction	Description
1.	#include<stdio.h>	Header file included
2.	#include<conio.h>	Header file included
3.	void main()	Execution of program begins
4.	{	String is declare with name str and size of storing 10 alphbates
5.	char str[10];	
6.	clrscr();	Clear the output of previous screen
7.	printf("enter a string");	Print "enter a string"
8.	scanf("%s",&str);	Entered string is stored at address of str
9.	printf("\n user entered string is %s",str);	Print: user entered string is (string entered by user)
10.	getch();	Used to hold the output screen
11.	}	Indicates end of scope of main function

Output :
    enter a string
    Roshan
    User enter string is Roshan

Following are the list of string manipulation function

Sr. No.	String Function	Purpose
1.	strcat	use to concatenate (append) one string to another
2.	strcmp	use to compare one string with another. (Note: The comparison is case sensitive)

3.	strchr	use to locate the first occurrence of a particular character in a given string
4.	strcpy	use to copy one string to another.
5.	strlen	use to find the length of a string in bytes,

3.14 User Define Data Types

C language provides three types of datatypes

1. **Fundamental Data type**: includes data types like int, char,float etc.
2. **Derived data type:** includes data types like array, pointer
3. **User define data type:** includes data types like Structure and Union

User define data type is define by user. User define data types are used to define different types of variable under one common name. There are two types of user define data type

    1. Structure: It is the user define data type. With the help of structure user can define different types of variables under the shelter of one common name. Syntax for defining structure is as follows

```
struct structure_name
{
    structure element1;
    structure element2;
    structure element2;
    :
    :
    structure element n;
};
```

In the above syntax 'struct' is a keyword, which is used to define the structure.

Structure name can be anything according to the rules of defining names of variable. Within curly brackets user can define the several variables.

Size of structure is the summation of size of all the elements of the structure.

User can access the elements of structure by creating the object of the structure.

2. Union: It is the user define data type. With the help of union user can define different types of variables under the shelter of one common name. Syntax for defining union is as follows

    union union _name

    {

        union element1;

        union element2;

        union element3;

        :

        :

        :

        union element n;

    };

In the above syntax union is a keyword, which is used to define the union.

union name can be anything according to the rules of defining names of variable. Within curly brackets user can define the several variables.

Size of union is the size of largest element of the union

User can access the elements of union by creating the object of the union.

The C Language Keywords

Auto	break	case	char	Const	continue	default	Do
double	else	enum	extern	Float	for	goto	If
Int	long	register	return	Short	signed	sizeof	static
Struct	switch	typedef	union	Unsigned	void	volatile	While

Multiple Choice Questions

1. Which of the following symbols is used to denote a pre-processor statement?
    A) !
    B) #
    C) ~
    D) ;
2. The preprocessor in C language is used for
    A) Processing the function calls
    B) Processing input and output statements

C) Processing the preprocessor directives

D) Processing all the statements in program

3. The declaration int a[10]; In c Language means

A) The value 10 is assigned to variable 'a'

B) It is character array which can store 10 characters

C) It is integer array which can store 10 integer values in an array

D) Both 'b' and 'c'

4. struct data type in C language is used for

A) Storing group of different data types

B) Storing group of same data type

C) Storing only one data type

D) all of the above

5. Symbolic constants can be defined using a_____

A) # define directive B) const keyword

C) symbolic notation D) None of these

6. A string is terminated by a _____ character, which is written as _____

A) blank, ' ' B) new line, \n

C) null, '\0' D) string, %s

7. Which expression reference to the 4th element of an array

A) num[4]; B) int a(4);

C) num(0-4); D) num[3];

8. Which of the following statements is true?

A) The array int num[27] has twenty six element

B) The expression num [0] designates the first element in the array.

C) It is necessary to initialize the array at the time of declaration.

D) The expression num[27] designates the twenty sixth element in the array

9. The expressions written in the ` for ` loop, are separated using a _____.

A) colon B) comma C) semicolon D) hyphen

10. malloc() function used in dynamic memory allocation is available in which header file?
    A) stdio.h   B) stdlib.h   C) conio.h   D) mem.h

11. int x[] = { 1, 4, 8, 5, 1, 4 };
    int *ptr, y;
    ptr = x + 4;
    y = ptr - x;
    What does y in the sample code above equal?
    A) -3   B) 0
    C) 4   D) 4 + sizeof(int)

12. Which symbol is used as a ` statement terminator ` in ` C ` ?
    A) !   B) #   C) ~   D) ;

13. Which among the following is a unconditional control structure ?
    A) do-while   B) if-else   C) goto   D) for

14. A "do... while " loop terminates, when the expression written in ` while ` returns _____
    A) 1   B) 0   C) -1   D) NULL

15. Which of the following is a keyword used for denoting a storage class?
    A) printf   B) external   C) auto   D) scanf

16. Which amongst the following is not a structured data type?
    A) Array   B) void   C) structure   D) union

17. Minimum number of temperory variables needed to exchange the contents of two variables is
    A) 1   B) 2   C) 3   D) 0

18. The body of a ` WHILE ` Loop has
    A) one statement only   B) atleast two statements
    C) one or more statements   D) None of above.

19. Determine which of the following is invalid numeric constant.
    A) 0.5   B) 27,822   C) 12345678   D) 0XBCFDAL

20. Which is not conditional and unconditional branching ?
    A) if   B) switch   C) break   D) include

Unit 3 | 3.21

21. Which of the following statement is correct ?
    A) C provides no input-output feature
    B) C provides no file access feature
    C) C provides no feature to manipulate composite objects
    D) All of above

22. The following statement print("%f",9/5); prints
    A) 1.8   B) 1   C) 2   D) none of these

23. which of the following is not a logical operator?
    A) &   B) &&   C) || D. !

24. How do printf() format specifiers %e and %f differ in their treatment of floating-point numbers?
    A) %e always displays an argument of type double in engineering notation; %f always displays an argument of type double in decimal notation
    B) %e expects a corresponding argument of type double; %f expects a corresponding argument of type float.
    C) %e displays a double in engineering notation if the number is very small or very large. Otherwise, it behaves like %f and displays the number in decimal notation.
    D) %e displays an argument of type double with trailing zeros; %f never displays trailing zeros.

25. Which of the following is not a character classification in the 'C' language?
    A) alphabets   B) characters
    C) digits   D) graphical

26. Consider following statments I] An array is variable which can store multiple elements of similar type. II] Structure contains similar data types together.
    A) I is correct   B) II is correct
    C) I & II are correct   D) None of above.

27. In "C" program, constant is defined
    A) before main   B) after main
    C) anywhwre   D) none of above

28. A character variable can at a time store maximum _____.
    A) 1 Byte   B) 4 Bytes   C) 8 Bytes   D) 16 Bytes

29. What is the meaning of 'while (1)'?
    A) Execution of loop only once   B) Execution of loop at least once
    C) Infinite Loop   D) No execution of the loop
30. Which of the following is not an integer constant in ` C ` language?
    A) –320   B) –14.05   C) 45   D) 1456
31. One of the following is not a character constant in ` C ` language. Identify it.
    A) ' '   B) 'bb'   C) d   D) '?'
32. Which one is not keyword?
    A) else   B) while   C) switch(choice)   D) for
33. Find the correct form of ` nested if `
    A) if(if(condition)) do this;
    B) else(if(condition) do this;
    C) if(condition) { if(condition) do this; }
    D) if&&if(condition)
34. Which symbol is used to separate multiple initialization in the 'for' loop?
    A) &&   B) ,
    C) ;   D) None of the above
35. The keyword .... allows to take the control to the beginning of the loop, by passing the statements inside the loop, which have not yet been executed.
    A) goto   B) for   C) continue   D) case
36. Which of the following loop is not used in ` C ` language?
    A) 'for' loop   B) 'if...else'
    C) 'Repeat...until' loop   D) 'do..while' loop
37. When the keyword _____ is encountered inside any 'C' loop, control automatically passes to the first statement after the loop.
    A) goto   B) break   C) default   D) continue
38. Which of the following 'for' statements is wrong?
    A) for(i=0, j=1;i<5;i++)   B) for(i=0;i<5;i++);
    C) for(i=0;i<5;i++);   D) for(;i>7;)
39. How many ` ; ` (semicolon) are included in ` for ` statement (or loop)?
    A) 0   B) 1   C) 2   D) 3

40. The _____ statement allows the programmer to take the control to the beginning of the loop, bypassing the statement inside the loop which has not yet been executed.

   A) while   B) continue   C) go to   D) if

41. Which of the following is a Scalar Data type?

   A) Float   B) Union   C) Array   D) Pointer

42. The _____ loop allows programmer to specify three things about a loop in single line.

   A) for   B) while   C) goto   D) switch

43. For using character function, we must include the header file _____ in the program.

   A) string.h   B) stdio.h   C) ctype.h   D) math.h

44. Which one of the following is a true statement about pointers?

   A) They are always 32-bit values.
   B) For efficiency, pointer values are always stored in machine registers.
   C) With the exception of generic pointers, similarly typed pointers may be subtracted from each other.
   D) A pointer to one type may not be cast to a pointer to any other type.

45. Which one of the following variable names is not valid?

   A) go_cart   B) go4it   C) 4season   D) run4

46. Which of the following is not a floating point constant in `C` language?

   A) 45.6   B) -31.8   C) pi   D) 40

47. The expression ` x != y ` is true if

   A) x is equal to y.
   B) x is not equal to y.
   C) x is less than or equal to y
   D) x is greater than or equal to y.

48. Which of the following is not a valid indentifier in `C` language?

   A) A3   B) B.A_4   C) if   D) IF

49. Which of the following statements about the ` switch ` statement is false?

   A) No two case labels can have the same value
   B) The switch control expression must be of 'character' type
   C) The case-labled constant can be a constant or a variable
   D) Two case labels can be associated with the same statement series

50. A two way selection is implemented in the program, by using _____ statement.
    A) case   B) else..if   C) switch   D) if..else

51. Header files in C contains
    A) Compiler commands
    B) Library functions
    C) Header information of C programs
    D) Operators for files

52. Which header file contains strlen() function?
    A) stdio.h   B) conio.h   C) string.h   D) math.h

53. Which statements is used to take the control to the beginning of the loop?
    A) exit   B) break   C) continue   D) no of these

54. Which of the following gives the memory address of a variable pointed to by pointer named as ` p ` ?
    A) p;   B) *p;   C) &p;   D) addressA);

55. An integer constant in C must have_____
    A) at least one digit
    B) at least one decimal point
    C) A comma along with digits
    D) Digits separated by commas

56. A 'do...while' loop is useful when we want that statement within the loop must be executed_____.
    A) only once   B) at least once
    C) more than once   D) none of above.

57. Which of the following gives the value stored in a pointer named as ` a ` ?
    A) a;   B) valA);   C) *a;   D) &a;

58. The real constant in C can be expressed in which of the following forms?
    A) Fractional form only
    B) Exponential form only
    C) ASCII form only
    D) both fractional and exponential forms

59. The statement char ch= 'Z' would store what in varaible named ` ch `
    _____

    A) the character Z

    B) ASCII value of Z

    C) Z along with single inverted commas

    D) both (1) & (2).

60. The maximum value that an integer constant can have is_____
    A) -32767   B) 32767
    C) 1.70E+38   D) -1.70E+38

61. Which of the following is not a valid character constant?
    A) 'thank you'   B) 'enter values of P,N,R'
    C) '23.56E-03'   D) all the above

62. If ` a ` is an integer variable, a=5/2; will initialise the variable ` a ` with the value____
    A) 2.5   B) 3   C) 2   D) 0

63. Which of the following is the correct output for the program given below?

    #include<stdio.h>
    void main()
    {
        int i=1;
        if(!i)
        printf("Recursive calls are painful\n");
        else
        { i=0;
    printf("Recursive calls are challenging

    A) Recursive calls are challenging. Recursive calls are painful.

    B) Recursive calls are painful. Recursive calls are challenging.

    C) Recursive calls are the challenging.

    D) The code prints Recursive calls are challenging. Recursive calls are challenging (infinitely?.)

64. In ` C ` a variable name can not contain_____
    A) blank spaces   B) hyphen
    C) decimal point   D) all the above

65. Which of the following symbol is used to denote a pre-processor statement?
    A) !   B) #   C) ~   D) ;
66. Which of the following gives the memory address of an integer variable 'a' ?
    A) *a;   B) a;   C) &a;   D) addressA);
67. Which of the following is the proper declaration of an integer pointer?
    A) int x;   B) int &x;   C) int x*;   D) int *x;
68. The _____ symbol is used to denote any function of an input/output device in the program flowchart.
    A) Flowlines
    B) Processing
    C) parallelogram
    D) Terminal.
69. A _____ Symbol is used in a flowchart to represent arithmetic and data movement instructions.
    A) Flowlines
    B) Processing
    C) Input/Output
    D) Terminal.
70. The _____ with arrowheads are used to indicate the flow of an operation, that is, the exact Sequence in which the instructions are to be executed.
    A) Flowlines   B) Processing   C) Decision   D) Terminal.
71. Which of the following shows the correct hierarchy of arithmetic operators in 'C' ?
    A) **,* or / ,- or +
    B) **, * or /, + or -
    C) **, /, *, +, -
    D) . / or *, - or +
72. The keyword _____ is followed by an integer or character constant.
    A) switch   B) case   C) for   D) void
73. What is the maximum size of a double variable?
    A) 1Byte   B) 4 Bytes   C) 8 Bytes   D) 16 Bytes
74. The size of a string variable is_____.
    A) 1 Byte
    B) 4 Bytes
    C) Size of String array
    D) None of these
75. The _____ logic is used to produce loops in program , depending on some condition.
    A) Iteration logic
    B) Selection logic
    C) Sequence logic
    D) Decision logic

76. What is meaning of a ' * ' symbol when used before a variable ?
    A) 'address of a variable
    B) location of a variable
    C) space of a variable
    D) value at an address
77. Which escape character can be used to begin a new line in ` C ` ?
    A) \a
    B) \b
    C) \m
    D) \n
78. Which of the following operators has the 2nd highest priority?
    A) =
    B) * / %
    C) + -
    D) ||
79. A character constant should be enclosed within a pair of ____
    A) Single quotes
    B) Double quotes
    C) Both a and b
    D) None of these
80. A string constant should be enclosed within a pair of _____
    A) Single quotes
    B) Double quotes
    C) Both a and b
    D) None of these
81. Which of the following is an invalid character constant?
    A) ')'
    B) '$'
    C) 'a'
    D) 'abc'
82. The maximum length of a variable in ` C ` programming language is _____
    A) 8
    B) 16
    C) 32
    D) 64
83. What is meaning of a '&' symbol when used before a variable?
    A) address of a variable
    B) value of a variable
    C) space of a variable
    D) name of a variable
84. To return control back to the calling program which keyword is used.?
    A) void
    B) return
    C) back
    D) None
85. Which operators are useful in pointer operators?
    A) #<include>
    B) #
    C) *and &
    D) None
86. If int s[5] is one dimentional array of integers which of the following refers to third element in an array?
    A) *(s+2)
    B) *(s+3)
    C) s+3
    D) s+2
87. Following are the not looping statements.
    A) if-then-else
    B) do-while
    C) repeat-until
    D) for loop
88. Structure is a collection of _____.
    A) Different data types
    B) Different constants.
    C) Different records.
    D) Same data types

Unit 3 | 3.28

89. Which of the following is not preprocessor directory?
    A) #if   B) #elseif   C) #undef   D) #pragma
90. To recive the string "We are the FE students", in an array char str[100], which of the following functions would you use?
    A) scanf("%s",str);   B) gets(str)
    C) getche(str)   D) getchar(str)
91. Which operator is used to access the structure element?
    A) *   B) .   C) ->   D) &
92. When we pass an array of a structure to a function it is passed by the_____ mechanism.
    A) Call by value   B) Call by reference
    C) Call by name   D) None
93. Unions are the _____
    A) Inbuilt data types   B) Derived Data types
    C) Data types   D) None
94. An integer constant in C must have _____ .
    A) Atleast one digit
    B) Atleast one decimal point
    C) A comma along with digits
    D) Digits seperated by commas
95. c = getchar(); What is the proper declaration for the variable c in the code?
    A) char *c;   B) unsigned int c;
    C) int c;   D) char c;
96. if int s[5] is a one dimensional array of integers, which of the following statements refers to the third element in the array?
    A) *(s+2)   B) *(s+3)   C) S+3   D) S+2
97. I/P devices are _____ .
    A) monitor, keyboard, mouse   B) keyboard, mouse, scanner,
    C) Joystick, trackball, digitizer   D) Both B and C
98. Constant is _____.
    A) Constant program code
    B) Constant variable declaration
    C) Both A and B
    D) Way to define variable that can not modified

99. Variable is _____ .
    A) Identifier used to represent specific type of information
    B) Name associated with memory location
    C) Varying program statements
    D) Both A and B
100. Which of following operators in 'C' does not associate from the left to right?
    A) +   B) ,   C) =   D) %
101. In an array declaration 'int arr[12]' the word arr represents the _____.
    A) Variable   B) string
    C) Array variable   D) none of these.
102. What will happen if you put too few elements in an array when you initialize it?
    A) Nothing
    B) Possible system malfunction
    C) Error message from the compiler
    D) Unused elements will be filled with 0's or garbage
103. Which header file is essential for using strcmp() function?
    A) string .h   B) strings.h   C) text.h   D) strcmp.h
104. What will happen if you assign a value to an element of an array whose subscript exceeds the size of array?
    A) Element will be set to zero.
    B) Nothing
    C) Other data may be overwritten
    D) Error message from compiler will occur
105. An Ampersand before the name of a variable denotes..................
    A) Actual Value   B) variable name
    C) Address   D) Data Type
106. When you pass an array as an argument to a function what actually gets passed?
    A) Address of array
    B) Value of the elements of array
    C) Address of first element of array
    D) Number of elements of array

107. Can we use logical operators in ` if-else ` statement?
    A) yes
    B) no
    C) error
    D) Both B and C
108. Which of following statements about ` for ` loop are correct?
    A) Index value is retained outside the loop
    B) Index value can be changed from within the loop
    C) Goto can be jump, out of the loop
    D) All of above
109. Which of the following operator has the highest precedence?
    A) *
    B) ==
    C) >=
    D) +
110. Which of the following operator has the highest priority?
    A) ++
    B) %
    C) +
    D) ||
111. The continue keyword cannot be used with
    A) for
    B) while
    C) do
    D) switch
112. An union in C language denotes
    A) memory location
    B) memory store
    C) memory screen
    D) None of these
113. Keywords are also called _____ .
    A) reserved words
    B) compiler words
    C) dictionary words
    D) programming words
114. Which of the following operator has the lowest priority?
    A) ++
    B) %
    C) +
    D) ||
115. A ` C ` variable can not start with
    A) an alphabet
    B) a number
    C) a special symbol other than underscore
    D) Both B and C
116. Which of the following is the correct syntax of for loop?
    A) for (initialization, condition, inc/ dec)
    B) for (initialization, condition, inc/dec) { { ------; ------; ------; ------; } }
    C) for (initialization; condition; inc/dec)
    D) None of these { ------; ------; }

Unit 3 | 3.31

117. String constants should be enclosed between _____ .
    A) Single quotes
    B) Double quotes
    C) A or B
    D) None of these

118. Which of the following is a correct way of representing a variable in `C` ?
    A) int 0ram;
    B) float _calculate;
    C) int if;
    D) int run#fast;

119. The _____ function is used to display the output on the screen.
    A) scanf
    B) printf
    C) getchar
    D) clrscr

120. There are how many loop constructs in `C` language ?
    A) 3
    B) 4
    C) 1
    D) 2

121. An array name is _____.
    A) an array variable
    B) a keyword
    C) a common name shared by all of its elements
    D) not use in program

122. An array is used to represent _____.
    A) list of integer data item
    B) list of real data type
    C) list of different data type
    D) list of data item of same data type

123. The _____ format string is used for displaying floating point number with an exponent.
    A) %d
    B) %f
    C) %e
    D) %g

124. How many loops are present in C?
    A) One
    B) Two
    C) Three
    D) None of these

125. If a static array of integers is not initialized ,the elements will hold default value……..
    A) 0
    B) 1
    C) a integer number
    D) the charcter constant '\0'

126. What is a preprocessor directive?
    A) It is a message from a compiler to the programmer
    B) It is a message from a compiler to the linker
    C) It is a message from a programmer to the preprocessor
    D) t is a message from a programmer to the microprocessor

127. The _____.enhances the versatility of the computer allowing it to perform a set of instructions repetedly.
    A) compiler
    B) loop l
    C) header files
    D) statement

128. Which of the following is iterative control structures?
    A) if statement
    B) if-else statement
    C) do-while loop
    D) goto statement

129. Which of the following control structures are used in an iteration logic _____.
    A) IF....THEN & IF...THEN...ELSE
    B) DO ..& WHILE
    C) DO..WHILE & REPEAT...UNTILL
    D) DO..WHILE & IF...ELSE

130. Explicit type conversion is known as _____.
    A) casting
    B) conversion
    C) disjunction
    D) separation

131. `C` variable can not start with_____
    A) an alphabet
    B) a number
    C) a special symbol other than underscore
    D) both B & C

132. In a while loop the parantheses after the 'while' contains a _____
    A) condition   B) statement   C) count   D) value

133. Keyword is _____ .
    A) Variable name
    B) Constant word used in 'C'
    C) Reserve character of 'C'
    D) All of above

Unit 3 | 3.33

134. `If-else` statement is used as _____ .
    A) Decision control structure   B) Conditional statements
    C) Repetition of code   D) Both B and C

135. I/P functions are _____ .
    A) getchar(), puts(), gets()   B) getchar(), scanf(), gets()
    C) Both A and B   D) None of above

136. Which of the following statement is correct related to an if-else statement ?
    A) If we use an if it is compulsory to use an else
    B) Every if-else can be replaced by ? : operator.
    C) Nested if-else is allowed.
    D) Only one if-else can be written.

137. C=getchar () is used for a _____ operation.
    A) Character input   B) character output
    C) String input   D) string output

138. putcharD) function is used for a _____ opearations.
    A) Character input   B) character output
    C) String input   D) string output

139. Which is the correct syntax of do while loop?
    A) do { ------; ------;.)
    B) do{ ------; ------;)
    C) do { while (condition) ------; ------;}
    D) None of these

140. Syntax of while loop is _____.
    A) while { (condition); ------; ------;
    B) while(condition) { ------; ------; }
    C) while {-----; ------; }(condition);
    D) none of these

141. Struct keyword is used to define ...
    A) array   B) string   C) union   D) structure

142. . ... is standard output function
    A) printf   B) scanf   C) getch   D) clrscr

143. Which of the following is keyword
    A) if   B) string   C) data type   D) None of these
144. For string data type ... format specifier is used
    A) %d   B) %c   C) %f   D) %s
145. When an ` if..else ` statement is included within an ` if ..else ` statement , it is known as a _____.
    A) Next if statement   B) another if statement
    C) combined if statement   D) Nested if statement
146. The ` *(&i) ` is stands for ,
    A) ' value at address ' operator   B) ' address of ' operator
    C) both A&B   D) none of above
147. Which of the following is an iterative control structure?
    A) If   B) if else   C) do while   D) go to
148. The size of the data type ` double ` in C programming language is _____
    A) 16 bits   B) 32 bits   C) 54 bits   D) 64 bits
149. Which of the following is a correct way of representing a variable in C?
    A) int 1ram;   B) float _calculate;
    C) int if;   D) int run#fast;
150. An integer constant in ` C ` must have
    A) At least one digit
    B) At least one decimal point
    C) A comma along with digits
    D) Digits separated by commas
151. The ` * ` operator stands for _____ .
    A) ' address of ' operator   B) ' value at address ' operator
    C) format specifier   D) both A&B
152. Which of the following is invalid variable name?
    A) BASICSALARY   B) _basic
    C) basic-hra   D) hELLO
153. Which of the following is NOT a character constant?
    A) 'Thank You'   B) 'Enter values of P, N, R'
    C) '23.56E-03'   D) All the above

154. A ` C ` variable cannot start with
    A) An alphabet
    B) A number
    C) A special symbol other than underscore
    D) Both B & C above

155. Which of the following statement is wrong?
    A) mes = 123.56 ;
    B) con = 'T' * 'A' ;
    C) this = 'T' * 20 ;
    D) 3 + a = b ;

156. A structure is a collection of_____ .
    A) different data types scattered throughout memory
    B) the same data type scattered throughout memory
    C) the same data type placed next to each other in memory
    D) different data types placed next to each other in memory

157. The variables which hold addresses of other variables are,
    A) array   B) structure   C) pointer   D) both A&C

158. What will be the output of the following code ?
    main()
    {
        int x=10,y=20;
        if(x==y)
        printf("\n%d%d",x,y);
    }
    A) 10,20
    B) No Output
    C) syntax error
    D) none of the above

159. A ` while ` loop is knowm as a
    A) exit controlled loop
    B) entry controlled loop
    C) exit controlled loop
    D) none of the above

160. Maximum no of elements in the array declaration int sss[5][8] is_____
    A) 28   B) 32   C) 35   D) 40

161. Pointer to pointers is a term used to describe
    A) pointers whose contents are the address of another pointer
    B) Any two pointers that point to the same variable
    C) Any two pointers that point to variables of the same type
    D) pointers used as formal parameters in a function header

162. An _____ is an integral value used to access an element in an array.
    A) constant   B) element   C) index   D) number
163. Which of the following file modes opens a file in the write state for updating?
    A) ab   B) a+b   C) rb   D) r+b
164. Which of these results when failure occurs during an open or during either a read or write operation related to file I/O ?
    A) error state   B) fail state   C) read state   D) update state
165. Which of the following C functions is used to set file pointer?
    A) fwrite   B) fseek   C) fread   D) putc
166. * is used to denote_____
    A) Pointer   B) Addition   C) Division   D) Assignment
167. Structure is a collection of _____elements
    A) Same
    B) Different
    C) Same or Different
    D) Same & Different
168. Pointer is nothing but_____
    A) address of variable
    B) int
    C) char
    D) value of variable
169. Character array is nothing but_____
    A) string   B) int   C) char   D) float
170. Which of the following statement transfers the control to the beginning of the loop?
    A) exit
    B) break
    C) continue
    D) None of the above
171. A ` do-while ` loop is useful when the statements within the loop must be executed:
    A) Only once
    B) At least once
    C) More than once
    D) None of the above
172. A case in ` switch ` statement is terminated by _____ if control should not fall through the successive cases.
    A) break   B) break;   C) ;   D) break,
173. The getch() function in ` C ` is _____
    A) user defined function
    B) library function
    C) both of above
    D) none of above

Unit 3 | 3.37

174. Which of the following is correct way of declaring a float pointer
    A) float ptr
    B) float *ptr
    C) *float ptr
    D) None of the above

175. Array can be initialized automatically, provided they are declared with following specifiers
    A) automatic
    B) external
    C) static
    D) both B & C

176. Which of the following ` C ` statement is syntactically correct?
    A) for( );
    B) for(;);
    C) for(;;)
    D) for(,);

177. Which one of the following is not a valid character specification for C language ?
    A) special character
    B) control
    C) digit
    D) space

178. In what sequence the initialization, testing and execution of the body is done in a ` do-while ` loop
    A) initialization, execution of the body, testing
    B) Execution of the body, initialization, testing
    C) nitialization, testing, execution of the body
    D) None of the above

179. int *my_pointer;
 int barny;
 my_pointer=&barny;
 *my_pointer=3;
 Study the above code and mark which is correct?
    A) value of barny becomes 3
    B) value of my_pointer remains unchanged;
    C) both A and B
    D) None of the above

180. A pointer is a _____
    A) derived data type
    B) user defined data type
    C) abstract data type
    D) all of the above

181. Difference between ` while ` and ` do-while `
    A) 'while' loop executes one or more times and 'do-while' executes zero or more times
    B) Both 'while' loop and 'do-while' executes one or more times
    C) Both 'while' loop and 'do-while' executes zero or more times
    D) 'while' loop executes zero or more times and 'do-while' executes one or more times

182. An array is a collection of _____
    A) a set of values with different data types scattered throughout the memory
    B) a set of values with the same data types scattered throughout the memory
    C) a set of values with the same data types placed next to each other in the memory
    D) a set of values with different data types placed next to each other in the memory

183. Which element of the array does the expression num[4] references, where `num` is a name of array?
    A) Forth   B) Third   C) Fifth   D) First

184. If you don't initialize a static array, with what value the elements will be initialised?
    A) 0
    B) an undetermined value
    C) -1
    D) the character constant ' \0'

185. The strncat() funtion is used _____ .
    A) to copy n characters of a string
    B) to compare n characters of a string
    C) to reverse the string
    D) none of these.

186. Which of the following is not a integer constant in `C`?
    A) 'C'   B) 123   C) 45   D) 1.2

187. Which of the following data types is not valid in a switch .. case statement?
    A) character   B) integer   C) enum   D) float

188. Any variable in C starts with a _____ .
    A) Number
    B) Keyword
    C) Alphabet
    D) None of the above

189. In C, the address of m's memory location can be determined by the expression
    A) *M   B) M&   C) &M   D) M*

190. Which among the following is a unconditional control structure?
    A) do-while   B) if-else   C) goto   D) for

191. A `continue` statement terminates a_____.
    A) function
    B) iteration
    C) body of a loop
    D) None of the above

192. Constants in `C` refer to _____
    A) A Fixed value that do not change during the execution of the program.
    B) A Fixed value that can change during the execution of the program.
    C) A Fixed value that can change after the compilation of the program.
    D) A Fixed value that can change after linking the program.

193. An array is the _____ data type.
    A) Primary
    B) User defined
    C) Derived
    D) Set

194. The syntax of the array declaration is:
    A) datatype nameofarray [size];
    B) nameofarray [size];
    C) datatype nameofarray ;
    D) all of above

195. If `a` is a variable defined in a `C` program then &a denotes the _____.
    A) content of a
    B) address of a
    C) Both A and B
    D) none of these

196. Which of the following statements determines whether the contents of string1 are same as contents of string2 or not?
    A) if (string1 == string2)
    B) if (string1, string2)
    C) if (strcmp(string1,string2) ==0)
    D) if (strcmp(string1, string2) < 0)

197. The _____ format specification is used to write a long integer variable.
    A) %d
    B) %dd
    C) %lf
    D) %ld

198. A `break` statement is used _____.
    A) to terminate a loop and execute the next statement
    B) to skip a loop and terminate the program
    C) to continue a loop and execute the next statement
    D) execute the next statement

199. Which of the following function is used to read the input from a string?
    A) scanf
    B) fscanf
    C) fprintf
    D) sscanf

200. In ` C `, a semicolon is used _____.
    A) to terminate a statement
    B) to break a loop
    C) to give a comment
    D) none of these
201. A ` switch ` statement is used to make a decision _____.
    A) to switch the processor to execute some other program
    B) between two alternatives
    C) amongst many alternatives
    D) none of these
202. When applied to a variable, what does the unary "&" operator yield?
    A) The variable's address
    B) The variable's right value
    C) The variable's binary form
    D) The variable's value
203. To delete a dynamically allocated array named `a`, the correct statement is
    A) delete a;
    B) delete a[0];
    C) delete []a;
    D) delete [0]a;
204. Identify the invalid keyword in the following list.
    A) integer
    B) char
    C) float
    D) long int
205. Which of the following is not a valid data type In ` C ` ?
    A) char
    B) float
    C) int
    D) logical
206. && is used as a _____
    A) operand
    B) Mathematical operator
    C) logical operator
    D) None of the above
207. What is the difference between declaration and a definition of a variable?
    A) Both can occur multiple times, but a declaration must occur first.
    B) There is no difference between them.
    C) A declaration occurs once, but a definition may occur many times.
    D) A definition occurs once, but a declaration may occur many times.
208. Array is the collection of ---------- data type.
    A) Disimilar
    B) Similar
    C) None of these
    D) two
209. A string is terminated by...............
    A) /n
    B) /t
    C) /0
    D) \0

Unit 3 | 3.41

210. Array passed as an argument to a function is interpreted as
    A) Address of the array
    B) Values of the first elements of the array
    C) Address of the first element of the array
    D) Number of element of the array
211. What is the size of a float variable in terms of number of bytes?
    A) 1 Byte   B) 2 Bytes   C) 4 Bytes   D) 8 Bytes
212. Is Nesting of if-else statements is possible ?
    A) Yes   B) NO   C) Can't say   D) None of these
213. What does a pointer variable store?
    A) Data   B) Address   C) Both A & B   D) None of these
214. The string is terminated by a _____ character
    A) '0'   B) '\0'   C) blank space   D) none
215. Which of the following is the correct way of declaring a float pointer ?
    A) Float ptr   B) Float *ptr   C) *float ptr   D) none
216. What does the "auto" specifier do?
    A) It automatically initializes a variable to 0;.
    B) It indicates that a variable's memory will automatically be preserved.
    C) It automatically increments the variable when used.
    D) It automatically initializes a variable to NULL.
217. Which of following functions compare two strings?
    A) strcpy()   B) strcp()   C) strcmp()   D) strcomp()
218. Syntax of for loop is initialization;----------------;increment/decrement
    A) value   B) limit
    C) less than/greater then   D) zero
219. The difference between getch() and getche() is _____.
    A) getch() gets a character and getche() gets a character and echo the received character
    B) Both perform similar job
    C) getche() gets a character and getch() gets a character and echo the received character
    D) None of above

| FPL – I ENGG. (F.E. SEM. I) | C PROGRAMMING |

220. Total no of keywords available in C are ____.
   A) 28   B) 36   C) 32   D) 26

221. If statement char ch= ` Z ` would store in ch_____
   A) The char
   B) ASCII value of Z
   C) Z along with single inverted commas
   D) the main() function

222. break statement can be simulated by using
   A) goto   B) return
   C) exit   D) any of the above features

223. A structure declaration _____.
   A) describes prototype   B) creates structure variables
   C) defines structure function   D) is not necessary

224. A Structure is a data type in where _____.
   A) each element must have same data type
   B) each element must have pointer type
   C) each element may have different data type
   D) no element is defined

225. The two dimensional array element are stored in a ____ form.
   A) column major order   B) row major
   C) both a & b   D) Random

226. The operation that can be performed on pointers are _____.
   A) adition or subtraction of pointers and integers
   B) assignment of pointer using pointer expression
   C) assignment of value 0 to pointer
   D) all above

227. The correct declaration statement of pointer variables p1,p2 is _____.
   A) int p1,p2   B) int *p1,p2;
   C) int p1,*p2;   D) int *p1,*p2

228. A pointer value refers to _____.
   A) an integer constant value   B) float value
   C) any value address in memory D) as an ordinary variable

Unit 3 | 3.43

229. A pointer variable may be assigned _____.
   A) An address value represented in hexadecimal
   B) An address value represented in octal
   C) an address of another variable
   D) an address value represented in binary

230. A union is a _____.
   A) special type of structure   B) pointer data type
   C) function data type   D) not a data type

231. A preprocessor directive statement should end with a
   A) semicolon   B) colon   C) nothing   D) comma

232. The function strcmp will return _____ if the two strings are same
   A) 1   B) any non zero integer
   C) -1   D) 0

233. If a ` while ` loop condition is checked for the seventh time, then the loop has already executed for _____ times.
   A) 0   B) 5   C) 6   D) 7

234. The maximum number of elements in array definition int x[10] is _____.
   A) 9   B) 19   C) 11   D) undefined

235. Identify the correct declaration of a 2-D array named ` a ` ?
   A) int a[10][10];   B) int a {[10][10];}
   C) int a(10) (10);   D) int a(10,10)

236. The number of elements that can be stored in an array is known by the _____.
   A) index value   B) index value
   C) array name   D) size of the array

237. A one dimensional array is also known as a _____.
   A) vector   B) table   C) matrix   D) array of array

238. When should we use an array?
   A) when we need to hold variable constant
   B) When we need to hold multiple data of same type
   C) When we need to obtain automatic memory cleanup functionality
   D) When we need to hold data of different data type

239. A structure definition _____.
    A) describes prototype   B) creates structure variables
    C) defines structure function D) is not necessary

240. In a ` for ` loop how many semicolons are allowed?
    A) greater than or equal to 2   B) exactly two
    C) 0,1 or 2   D) any number

241. Which statement can stop a loop?
    A) continue   B) break   C) initialization   D) if

242. Missing condition in while loop will generate a _____.
    A) compiler error   B) runtime error
    C) warning   D) infinite loop

243. Missing condition in a for loop will generate a _____.
    A) compiler error   B) runtime error
    C) warning   D) infinite loop

244. Pointers can be used to achieve a _____.
    A) call by function   B) call by reference
    C) call by name   D) call by procedure

245. A union differs from a structure in the following way
    A) all members are used at a time
    B) only one member can be used at a time
    C) union can not have more members
    D) union initializes all members as structure

246. In a worst case how many times a ` while ` loop executes?
    A) 0   B) 1   C) n times   D) infinite

247. Which of the following is the correct output for the program given below?
    main()
    {
        int k,num=30;
        k=(num>5?(num<=10? 100:200):500);
        printf("%d",k);
    }
    A) 200   B) 30   C) 100   D) 500

248. Constant and variables in C are of the type_____
    A) integer   B) float   C) character   D) all of these

Unit 3 | 3.45

249. The address of variable ex is obtained by using
    A) address(ex);   B) *ex;
    C) address(*ex);   D) &ex;
250. Preprocessor performs preliminary operations on
    A) Object files   B) Files to be compiled
    C) Linked files   D) Files to be executed
251. language of zeros and ones is called as _____ language
    A) Binary   B) Unary   C) Programming   D) All
252. Processor can understand only _____

    A) Binary   B) Unary   C) Programming   D) All
253. The zero in binary language represents the _____ of power supply
    A) Presence   B) Absence   C) Both   D) None
254. The one in binary language represents the _____ of power supply
    A) Presence   B) Absence   C) Both   D) None
255. C language was developed by _____
    A) Dennis Ritchie   B) Bjarne
    C) Microsoft   D) James Gosling
256. C language was developed in year _____
    A) 1990   B) 1970   C) 1922   D) 1972
257. C language was developed at_____
    A) Bell   B) Dell   C) Oracle   D) None
258. C language follows _____ oriented programming approach
    A) Object   B) Structure   C) Both   D) None
259. C is a _____ oriented language
    A) procedure   B) Object   C) Both   D) None
260. In C language, complete program is composed of various _____
    A) functions   B) procedures   C) Both   D) None
261. C language follows _____ approach in program design
    A) Bottom-up   B) Top-Down   C) Both   D) None
262. C is _____ programming language
    A) case sensitive   B) case insensitive
    C) Both   D) None

263. _____ compiler is required to execute the programs of C language
    A) Ansi   B) Antic   C) Turbo C   D) None
264. # is _____
    A) preprocessor   B) Compiler
    C) Header File   D) None
265. stdio.h is _____
    A) preprocessor   B) Compiler
    C) Header File   D) None
266. conio.h _____
    A) preprocessor B) Compiler C) Header File D) None
267. _____ is used to comment the block of instructions
    A) //   B) \\   C) ##   D) /* --- */
268. _____ is the output function
    A) printf   B) scanf   C) void   D) main
269. _____ is the input function
    A) printf   B) scanf   C) void   D) main
270. _____ function is used to to clear the output of previous program
    A) printf   B) scanf   C) clrscr   D) main
271. _____ function is used to hold output screen
    A) printf   B) scanf   C) getch   D) main
272. _____ key is used to compile the C program
    A) Alt+F9   B) ctrl+F9   C) F2   D) None
273. _____ key is used to execute the C program
    A) Alt+F9   B) ctrl+F9   C) F2   D) None
274. _____ key is used to save the C program
    A) Alt+F9   B) ctrl+F9   C) F2   D) None
275. _____ are used to define the scope of main function.
    A) {}   B) ()   C) []   D) None
276. _____ is also responsible to define type of variable
    A) Keyword   B) Datatype   C) identifier   D) None
277. %d inside scanf function indicates that the value entered by the user is considered as _____ value
    A) integer   B) float   C) character   D) double

278. %c inside scanf function indicates that the value entered by the user is considered as _____ value
    A) integer   B) float   C) character   D) double
279. %f inside scanf function indicates that the value entered by the user is considered as _____ value
    A) integer   B) float   C) character   D) double
280. _____ is used for new line
    A) \a   B) \n   C) \b   D) \t
281. _____ is used for audible alert
    A) \a   B) \n   C) \b   D) \t
282. _____ is used for back space
    A) \a   B) \n   C) \b   D) \t
283. _____ is used to give horizontal tab
    A) \a   B) \n   C) \b   D) \t
284. Keyword _____ is used to declare the quantity as a constant
    A) const   B) fasten   C) stable   D) fix
285. _____ data type allocate 2 bytes of memory
    A) int   B) float   C) char   D) double
286. _____ data type allocate 1 bytes of memory
    A) int   B) float   C) char   D) double
287. _____ data type allocate 4 bytes of memory
    A) int   B) float   C) char   D) double
288. _____ data type allocate 8 bytes of memory
    A) int   B) float   C) char   D) double
289. int data type supports the values in the range of_____
    A) -32768 to +32767   B) -128 to 127
    C) $3.4\ e^{-38}$ to $3.4\ e^{+38}$ D) $1.7\ e^{-308}$ to $1.7\ e^{+308}$
290. char data type supports the values in the range of_____
    A) -32768 to +32767   B) -128 to 127
    C) $3.4\ e^{-38}$ to $3.4\ e^{+38}$ D) $1.7\ e^{-308}$ to $1.7\ e^{+308}$
291. float data type supports the values in the range of_____
    A) -32768 to +32767   B) -128 to 127
    C) $3.4\ e^{-38}$ to $3.4\ e^{+38}$ D) $1.7\ e^{-308}$ to $1.7\ e^{+308}$

292. double data type supports the values in the range of_____
    A) -32768 to +32767   B) -128 to 127
    C) $3.4\ e^{-38}$ to $3.4\ e^{+38}$ D) $1.7\ e^{-308}$ to $1.7\ e^{+308}$
293. Access specifier for int data type is _____
    A) %d   B) % c   C) %f   D) %u
294. Access specifier for float data type is _____
    A) %d   B) % c   C) %f   D) %u
295. Access specifier for char data type is _____
    A) %d   B) % c   C) %f   D) %u
296. Access specifier for unsigned int data type is _____
    A) %d   B) % c   C) %f   D) %u
297. _____special symbol can be used in variable name
    A) #   B) _   C) -   D) %
298. Variable name should not start with_____
    A) Alphabet   B) Digit   C) Special Symbol   D) both B and C
299. _____ variable are only accessible in the block of code in which they are declared.
    A) Local   B) Global   C) Both   D) None
300. _____ variable are only accessible throughout the program.
    A) Local   B) Global   C) Both   D) None
301. _____ are the special words which have its pre-define meaning in C language
    A) Identifier   B) Keyword   C) variable   D) constant
302. There are total _____ keywords in C language
    A) 32   B) 35   C) 38   D) 52
303. Main is_____
    A) variable   B) Keyword   C) Both   D) None
304. _____ are the non executable part of program.
    A) Comments   B) function   C) array   D) none
305. _____ are used to find reminder of the division of two operand
    A) /   B) %   C) *   D) &
306. _____ operator are useful in performing mathematical calculations
    A) Arithmetic   B) Relational   C) Logical   D) Assignment

Unit 3 | 3.49

307. _____ are used to compare logical values of two operands.
   A) Arithmatic   B) Relational   C) Logical   D) Assignment
308. _____ operator is used to assign the value to variable
   A) Arithmatic   B) Relational   C) Logical   D) Assignment
309. _____ operator is used to compare two operands
   A) Arithmatic   B) Relational   C) Logical   D) Assignment
310. _____ operators are work on the each bits of data
   A) Bitwise   B) Relational   C) Logical   D) Assignment
311. _____ statements are used to select one option among the several other options
   A) Branching   B) looping   C) Both   D) None
312. _____ statements are used to repeat the block of code
   A) Branching   B) looping   C) Both   D) None
313. _____ is/are the example of branching statement
   A) if   B) switch   C) Both   D) None
314. _____ is/are the example of looping statement
   A) while   B) for   C) Both   D) None
315. _____ is responsible to read data according to the format specified in function
   A) scanf   B) gets   C) getchar   D) none
316. _____ function is responsible to read a string of text from the keyboard
   A) scanf   B) gets   C) getchar   D) none
317. _____ function is responsible to read a single character from the keyboard
   A) scanf   B) gets   C) getchar   D) none
318. _____ use to define constants or any macro substitution
   A) #define   B) #include   C) #if --   D) #endif
319. _____ use to includes a file into code.
   A) #define   B) #include   C) #if --   D) #endif
320. _____ use to evaluates a constant integer expression.
   A) #define   B) #include   C) #if --   D) #endif
321. _____ use to terminates conditional text
   A) #define   B) #include   C) #if --   D) #endif
322. _____ is linear data structure
   A) array   B) Tree   C) Graph   D) All

323. Indexing of array starts with _____
    A) 1   B) 2   C) 3   D) 0
324. _____ are called as the array of character
    A) String   B) Pointer   C) Tree   D) Graph
325. Access specifier for string is_____
    A) %d   B) %v   C) %s   D) None
326. built in functions for string are stored in_____ header file
    A) stdio.h   B) conio.h   C) string.h   D) math.h
327. _____ use to concatenate (append) one string to another
    A) strcat   B) strcmp   C) strchr   D) strcpy
328. _____ use to compare one string with another
    A) strcat   B) strcmp   C) strchr   D) strcpy
329. _____ use to locate the first occurrence of a particular character in a given string
    A) strcat   B) strcmp   C) strchr   D) strcpy
330. _____ use to copy one string to another
    A) strcat   B) strcmp   C) strchr   D) strcpy
331. _____ use to find the length of a string in bytes
    A) strlen   B) strcmp   C) strchr   D) strcpy
332. _____ is User define data type
    A) Structure   B) Union   C) Both   D) None
333. _____ data types are used to define different types of variable under one common name
    A) User define   B) Fundamental   C) Both   D) None

Answers

1.	B	2.	C	3.	C	4.	A	5.	B
6.	C	7.	D	8.	B	9.	C	10.	B
11.	C	12.	D	13.	C	14.	B	15.	C
16.	B	17.	D	18.	C	19.	B	20.	B
21.	C	22.	A	23.	A	24.	A	25.	D
26.	A	27.	C	28.	A	29.	C	30.	B

31.	C	32.	C	33.	C	34.	B	35.	C
36.	C	37.	B	38.	C	39.	C	40.	B
41.	C	42.	A	43.	A	44.	C	45.	C
46.	C	47.	B	48.	C	49.	B	50.	D
51.	B	52.	C	53.	C	54.	A	55.	A
56.	B	57.	C	58.	D	59.	A	60.	B
61.	D	62.	C	63.	C	64.	D	65.	B
66.	C	67.	D	68.	C	69.	B	70.	A
71.	B	72.	B	73.	C	74.	C	75.	A
76.	D	77.	D	78.	C	79.	A	80.	B
81.	D	82.	A	83.	A	84.	B	85.	C
86.	A	87.	A	88.	A	89.	B	90.	A
91.	B	92.	B	93.	B	94.	A	95.	D
96.	A	97.	D	98.	D	99.	D	100.	C
101.	C	102.	D	103.	A	104.	D	105.	C
106.	C	107.	A	108.	D	109.	A	110.	A
111.	D	112.	B	113.	A	114.	D	115.	D
116.	D	117.	B	118.	B	119.	B	120.	A
121.	C	122.	D	123.	C	124.	C	125.	A
126.	C	127.	B	128.	C	129.	C	130.	A
131.	D	132.	A	133.	C	134.	A	135.	B
136.	C	137.	A	138.	B	139.	D	140.	B
141.	D	142.	A	143.	A	144.	D	145.	D
146.	A	147.	C	148.	D	149.	B	150.	A
151.	B	152.	C	153.	D	154.	D	155.	D
156.	D	157.	C	158.	B	159.	B	160.	D
161.	A	162.	C	163.	B	164.	A	165.	B

166.	A	167.	C	168.	A	169.	A	170.	C
171.	B	172.	B	173.	B	174.	B	175.	D
176.	C	177.	B	178.	A	179.	C	180.	A
181.	D	182.	C	183.	C	184.	A	185.	A
186.	D	187.	D	188.	C	189.	C	190	C
191.	B	192.	A	193.	C	194.	A	195.	B
196.	C	197.	D	198.	A	199.	D	200.	A
201.	C	202.	A	203.	A	204.	A	205.	D
206.	C	207.	C	208.	A	209.	D	210.	C
211.	C	212.	A	213.	B	214.	B	215.	B
216.	B	217.	C	218.	B	219.	A	220.	C
221.	B	222.	A	223.	A	224.	C	225.	B
226.	D	227.	D	228.	C	229.	D	230.	A
231.	C	232.	D	233.	C	234.	B	235.	A
236.	D	237.	A	238.	B	239.	B	240.	B
241.	B	242.	A	243.	D	244.	B	245.	B
246.	A	247.	A	248.	D	249.	D	250.	B
251.	A	252.	A	253.	B	254.	A	255.	A
256.	D	257.	A	258.	B	259.	A	260.	C
261.	B	262.	A	263.	C	264.	A	265.	C
266.	C	267.	D	268.	A	269.	B	270.	C
271.	C	272.	A	273.	B	274.	C	275.	A
276.	B	277.	A	278.	C	279.	B	280.	B
281.	A	282.	C	283.	D	284.	A	285.	A
286.	C	287.	B	288.	D	289.	A	290.	B
291.	C	292.	D	293.	A	294.	C	295.	B
296.	D	297.	B	298.	D	299.	A	300.	B

301.	B	302.	A	303.	A	304.	A	305.	B
306.	A	307.	C	308.	D	309.	B	310.	A
311.	A	312.	B	313.	C	314.	C	315.	A
316.	B	317.	C	318.	A	319.	B	320.	C
321.	D	322.	A	323.	D	324.	A	325.	C
326.	C	327.	A	328.	B	329.	C	330.	D
331.	A	332.	C	333.	C						

C PROGRAMMING

Syllabus

Control Structure – Conditional and Unconditional Branching, Using if, switch, break, continue, go to and return statements;

Loop Structure – Creating Pretest Loops using for and while Statements. Creating Post test Loops using "do...while" statements.

Functions – Creating subprograms using Functions. Parameter Passing by value; Parameter Passing by reference. Main Function with argv, argc[]. Definition of Testing & Debugging.

4.1 Introduction to Control Structure

Control structure is an important concept in high level programming languages. Control structures are the instruction or the group of instructions in the programming language which are responsible for determining the sequence of other instructions in the program. Control structure is used for the reusability of the code. Control structure is useful when the program demands to repeatedly execute block of code for specific number of times or till certain condition is satisfied. Control structures can control the flow of execution of program based on some conditions. Following are the advantages of using control structures in C language.

- Increases reusability of code
- Reduces complexity, improves clarity, and facilitates debugging and modification.
- Easy to define in flowcharts.
- Control statements are also useful in the indentation of the program.

There are two types of control statements

1. Conditional Branching: In conditional branching decision point is based on the run time logic. Conditional branching makes use of both selection logic and iteration logic. In conditional branching flow of program is transfer when the specified condition is satisfied.

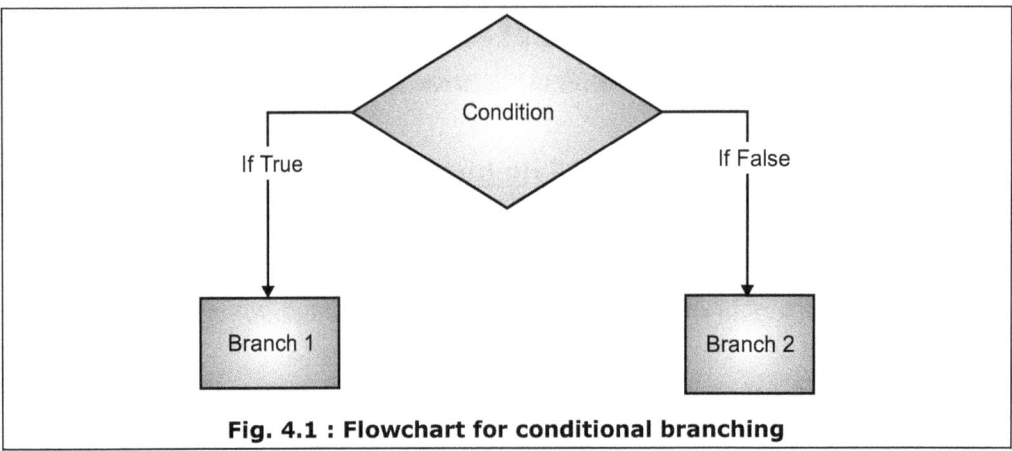

Fig. 4.1 : Flowchart for conditional branching

2. Unconditional Branching: In Unconditional branching flow of program is transferred to a particular location without concerning the condition. Unconditional branching makes use of sequential logic. In unconditional branching flow of program is transferred as per the instruction.

4.1.1 Conditional Branching

In conditional branching, change in sequence of statement execution depends upon the specified condition. Conditional statements allow programmer to check a condition and execute certain parts of code depending on the result of conditional expression. Conditional expression must be resulted into Boolean value. In C language, there are two forms of conditional statements:

1. **if-----else statement**: It is used to select one option between two alternatives.

2. **switch statement**: It is used to select one or more options between multiple alternative

4.1.1.1 Basic Structure of Selection Logic

This statement permits the programmer to allocate condition on the execution of a statement. If the evaluated condition is found to be true, the single statement following the "if" is execute. If the condition is found to be false, the following statement is skipped. Syntax of the 'if' statement is as follows

```
            if(condition)
                statement1
                statement2
```

In the above syntax, "if" is the keyword and condition in parentheses must evaluate to true or false. If the condition is satisfied (true) then compiler will execute statement1 and then statement 2. If the condition is not satisfied (false) then compiler will skip statement1 and directly execute statement 2.

if-----else statement:

This statement permits the programmer to execute a statement out of the two statements. If the evaluated condition is found to be true, the single statement following the "if" is executed and statement following else is skipped. If the condition is found to be false, statement following the "if" is skipped and statement following else is executed.

In this statement "if" part is compulsory whereas "else" is the optional part. For every "if" statement there may be or may not be "else" statement but for every "else" statement there must be "if" part otherwise compiler will gives "*Misplaced else*" error.

Syntax of the "if----else" statement is as follows

```
            if (condition)
                statement1;
            else
                statement2;
```

In the above syntax, "if" and "else" are the keywords and condition in the parentheses must evaluate to true or false. If the condition is satisfied (true) then compiler will execute statement1 and skip statement2. If the condition is not satisfied (false) then compiler will skip statement1 and directly execute statement2.

Nested if-----else statements:

Nested "if-----else" statements are used when programmer wants to check multiple conditions. Nested "if---else" contains several "if---else" a statement out of which only one statement is executed. Number of "if----else" statements is equal to the number of conditions to be checked. Following is the syntax for nested "if---else" statements for three conditions

```
            if (condition1)
                statement1;
```

```
            else if (condition2)
                statement2;
            else if (condition3)
                statement3;
            else
                statement4;
```

In the above syntax, compiler first checks condition 1, if it is true then it will execute statement 1 and skip all the remaining statements. If condition 1 is false then compiler directly checks condition 2, if it is true then compiler execute statement 2 and skip all the remaining statements. If condition 2 is also false then compiler directly checks condition 3, if it is true then compiler executes statement 3 otherwise it will execute statement 4.

4.1.1.2 Switch Statements

This statement permits the programmer to choose one or more option out of several options depending on one condition. When the switch statement is executed, the expression in the switch statement is evaluated and the control is transferred directly to the group of statements whose "case" label value matches with the value of the expression. Syntax for switch statement is as follows:

```
            switch(expression)
            {
                    case constant1:
                    statements 1;
                    break;
                    case constant2:
                    statements 2;
                    break;
                    ................. . .
                    default:
                    statements n;
                    break;
            }
```

In the above, "switch", "case", "break" and "default" are keywords. Out of which "switch" and "case" are the compulsory keywords whereas "break" and "default" are the optional keywords.

- "switch" keyword is used to start switch statement with conditional expression.
- "case" is the compulsory keyword which labeled with a constant value. If the value of expression matches with the case value then statement followed by "case" statement is executed.
- "break" is the optional keyword in switch statement. The execution of "break" statement causes the transfer of flow of execution outside the "switch" statements scope. Absence of "break" statement causes the execution of all the following "case" statements without concerning value of the expression.
- "default" is the optional keyword in "switch" statement. When the value of expression is not match with the any of the "case" statement then the statement following "default" keyword is executed.

4.1.2 Unconditional Branching

In unconditional branching, statements are executed without concerning the condition. Unconditional statements allow programmer to transfer the flow of execution to any part of the program. In C language, there are four types of unconditional statements:

1. Break statement: It is the unconditional jump instruction. It is used mainly with "switch" and loop statements. The execution of "break" instruction, transfer the flow of program outside the loop or "switch" statement Syntax of "break" statement is as follows

```
break;
```

When "break" statement is used inside the loops then execution of "break" statement causes the immediate termination of loop and compiler will execute next statement after the loop body.

2. Goto statement: "goto" statement is used to transfer the flow of program to any part of the program. The syntax of "go_to" statement is as follows

```
goto    label_name;
```

In the above syntax "goto" is a keyword which is used to transfer the flow of execution to the label specified after it. Label is an identifier that is used to mark the target statement to which the control is transferred. The target statement must be labeled and the syntax is as follows

```
label name :    statement;
```

In the above syntax label name can be anything but it should be same as that of name of the label specified in "goto" statement, a colon must follow the label. Each labeled statement within the function must have a unique label, i.e., no two statements can have the same label.

3. **Continue statement:** It is used mainly with "switch" and "loop" statements. The execution of "continue" instruction, skips the execution of remaining statements of the loop and transfers the flow of program to the loop control instruction. Syntax of "continue" statement is as follows

```
continue;
```

4. **Return statement:** The "return" statement terminates the execution of the current function and return control to the calling function. The "return" statement immediately ends the function, ignoring everything else in the function after it is called. It immediately returns to the calling function and continue from the point that it is called. Return also able to "return" a value which can be use in the calling function.

4.2 Loop Structure

This statement permits the programmer to write a statement or group of statements one time and execute it for multiple times. When the statements are repeated for a particular number of times then that loop is known as **count loop.** When the statements are repeated till some event is about to come across then that loop is known as **event loop**. Loop consists of three main statements

- **Initialization:** These statements are used to initialize loop variables. In these statements some initial value is assign to loop variables.
- **Condition:** These statements are used to terminate loop execution. In these statements some conditional/ final value is assign to loop variables.
- **Incrementation / Decrementation:** The execution of loop start from initial value to the final value. During each iteration of loop incrementation / decrementation statements are used to change the value of loop variable as per defined order .

There are two types of loops

1. **Pretest loop:** In this loop condition is check before the execution of loop statements.

2. **Posttest loop:** As name suggest, initially loops is executed for one time and then the condition is checked.

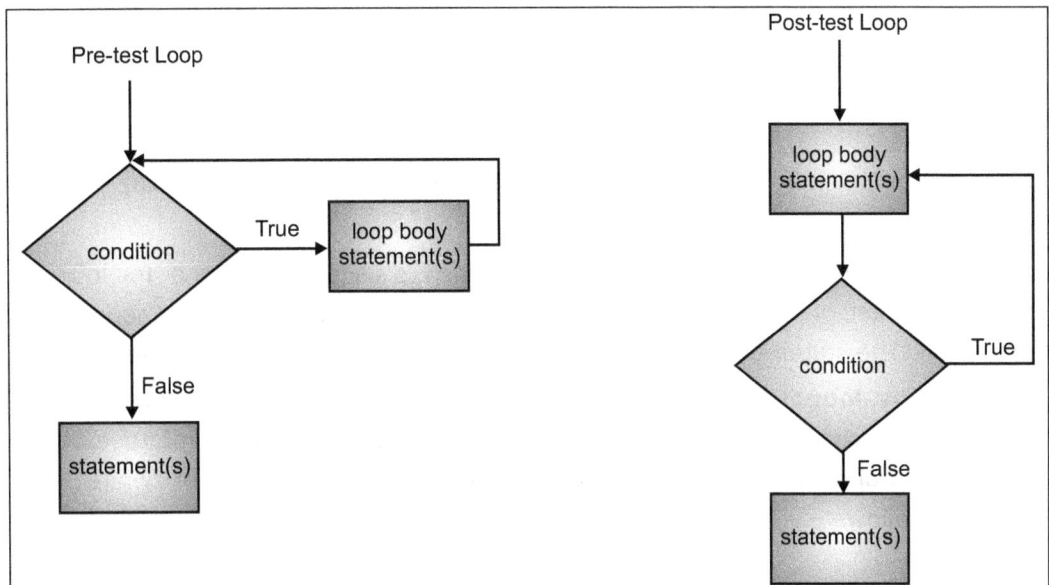

4.2.1 Pretest loop Structure

In pretest loops, the condition is checked before the execution of loop. In this type of loop, execution of loop completely depends upon the conditional statements. This type of loop is also called as "*Entry Controlled Loop*". Programmer can use one or more loops in another loop, this concept is known as *nested loops*. Following are the example of pretest loop

- **For loop:** "for" loop is the entry controlled loop, comes under the category of count loop. Following are the steps included in the execution of "for" loop
    1. Firstly the value of loop variable is initialized.
    2. Value of conditional variable is evaluated.
    3. If the condition is satisfied then the statements inside the loop are executed. Otherwise compiler will not execute the loop body statement and start execution from the statement next to body of the loop.
    4. After the execution of loop body statements, incrementation or decrementation of the variable is performed. This statement allows programmer to update loop control variables.

5. Steps 2, 3 and 4 are repeated each time till the condition is satisfied.

The syntax of for loop is as follows

```
for (initialization; condition; updation)
{
    Statement 1;
    Statement 2;
    ............
    Statement n;
}
```

In the above syntax "for" is a keyword which is used to start the 'for loop'. The circular bracket of for loop contains three loop statements which are separated by semicolon. The statements inside curly brackets are known as *body* of the loop.

- **While loop:** This loop statement allows programmer to execute a block of code repeatedly. 'while' loop is used when programmer want to execute a block of code repeatedly according to condition. The syntax of "while" loop is as follows

```
while ( condition)
{
    Statement 1;
    Statement 2;
    ............
    Statement n;
}
```

In the above syntax "while" is a keyword. This loop executes as long as the condition between parentheses after "while" is true. When condition is not satisfied, execution continues with the statement following the loop body. The condition is checked at the beginning of the loop, so if it is initially false, the loop statements will not be executed.

4.2.2 Post Test Loop Structure

In post test loops, the condition is checked after the first iteration of the loop. In this type of loop, execution of second and onwards iteration is completely depended upon the conditional statements. This type of loop is also called as "*Exit controlled*

Loop". Programmer can use one or more loops inside any another loop, this concept is known as nested loops. Following is the example of post test loop.

Do While loop: This loop statement execute a block of code for one time though the condition is false. This loop is used when programmer want to execute a block of code repeatedly with checked condition after the first iteration of the loop statements. The syntax of while loop is as follow

```
do
{
    Statement 1;
    Statement 2;
    ............
    Statement n;
}
while ( condition);
```

In the above syntax "do" and "while" are the keyword. During the execution of this loop, compiler initially executes all the statements inside the body of "do" part (ie from statements 1 to n sequentially). After the execution of statement, compiler will check the condition inside 'while" part. If the condition is satisfied the compiler again executes the "do" part of the loop. This process continues till the condition inside "while" part is true.

4.3 Functions

Similar to other languages C language also provides the facility of functions. Function is a block of code which is used to perform a specific task. In C language the complete program is composed of function.

Functions are useful to divide C programs into smaller modules. Programmer can invoke these modules anywhere inside C program for any number of times.

Functions are used to increase readability of the code. Size of program can be reduced by using functions. By using functions, programmer can divide complex tasks into smaller manageable tasks and test them independently before using them together.

Functions of C language are defined with the type of function. The type of functions indicates the data type of value which will return by function. In order to use functions in the program, initially programmer have to inform compiler about the functions. This is also called as defining a function. (Function Definition declaration).

In C programme all the function definitions are present outside the main function. All function need to be declared and defined before use. Function declaration requires function name, argument list, and return type.

The syntax for defining a function is as follows.

```
            Return Type  Function name (Argument list)
            {
                    Statement 1;
                    Statement 2;
                    ............ . . .
                    Statement n;
            }
```

In the above syntax, return type indicates the data type of value return by the function. If return type is not written then by default "int" data type is consider.

- Function name can be any alphanumeric value which is satisfying the rules used to define variable name and can be as long as 31 characters.
- The argument list is a formal list that includes data type and variable name combination. Each argument must be separated by comma.
- The body of the function describes what the function is supposed to do. The body starts with an opening curly bracket "{" and ends with a closing curly bracket "}".
- Everything between these two curly brackets belongs to the function.

There are two types of functions in c language.

1. Library Functions

A function which is predefined in C language is called library function. Library function is also called as **built in** function of C language. The definition of library function is stored in respective header file. Library functions are used to perform dedicated operation like taking input from user, displaying output, string handling operation, etc. Library functions are readily available and programmer can directly use it without writing any extra code. For example, printf () and scanf () are library function and their definition is stored in 'stdio' header file.

2. User Defined Functions

User define function is the block of code written by programmer to perform a particular task. As compiler doesn't have any idea about the user defined function, so programmer has to define and declare these functions inside the program body.

Programmer can define these function outside the main function but declaration of user define function should present in main function only. Whenever compiler executes function call (function declaration) then compiler shift the flow of program execution to the definition part of user define function.

Example

```
#include <stdio.h>
#include<conio.h>
int add (int x, int y)
{
   int sum;
   sum = x + y;
   return (sum);
}
main ()
{
   int a,b,c;
   a = 15;
   b = 25;
   c = add(a,b);
   printf ("\n Addition is %d ", c);
}
```

Output:

Addition is 40

There are two ways to pass the parameters to the function

1. **Parameter Passing by value**

   In this mechanism, the value of the parameter is passed while calling the function.

2. **Parameter Passing by reference**

   In this mechanism, the address of the parameter is passed while calling the function.

4.3.1 Parameter Passing by Value

This is the default way of passing the parameters to the function. This is achieved by passing the copy of data to the function. This mechanism is also called as call *by value*. In case of parameter passing by value, the changes made to the formal arguments in the called function have no effect on the values of actual arguments in the calling function.

This mechanism is used when programmer don't want to change the value of passed parameters. When parameters are passed by value then functions in C create copies of the passed in variables and requires processing on these copied variables.

Pass-by-value is implemented by actual data transfer so additional storage is required to maintain the copies of passed parameters.

Example:

```
#include <stdio.h>
#include<conio.h>
/* function declaration goes here.*/
void swap( int p1, int p2);
int main()
{
   int a = 10;
   int b = 20;
   printf("Before: Value of a = %d and value of b = %d\n",a,b);
   swap( a, b );
   printf("After: Value of a = %d and value of b = %d\n", a,b);
   getch();
}
void swap( int p1, int p2)
{
   int t;
   t = p2;
   p2 = p1;
   p1 = t;
   printf("Value of a(p1) = %d and value of b(p2) =%d\n",p1,p2);
}
```

Output :

Before: Value of a = 10 and value of b = 20

Value of a (p1) = 20 and value of b (p2) = 10

After: Value of a = 10 and value of b = 20

Note: In the above example the values of "a" and "b" remain unchanged before calling swap function and after calling swap function.

4.3.2 Parameter Passing by reference

This mechanism is used when programmer want a function to do the changes in passed parameters and reflect those changes back to the calling function. This mechanism is also called as call *by reference*. This is achieved by passing the address of variable to the function and function body can directly work over the addresses. Advantage of pass by reference is efficiency in both time and space. Whereas disadvantages are access to formal parameters is slow and inadvertent and erroneous changes may be made to the actual parameter.

Example:

```
#include <stdio.h>
#include<conio.h>
void swap( int *p1, int *p2);
int main()
{
   int a = 10;
   int b = 20;
   printf("Before:Value of a - %d and value of b = %d\n", a, b);
   swap( &a, &b);
   printf("After: Value of a = %d and value of b = %d\n", a, b);
}
void swap( int *p1, int *p2)
{
   int t;
   t = *p2;
   *p2 = *p1;
   *p1 = t;
   printf("Valueof a(p1)= %d and value of b(p2)=%d\n",*p1, *p2);
}
```

Output :

Before: Value of a = 10 and value of b = 20

Value of a (p1) = 20 and value of b(p2) = 10

After: Value of a = 20 and value of b = 10

Note: In the above example the values of "a" and "b" are changes after calling swap function.

4.4 Main Functions

In most of the programming languages, the "main" function indicates the starting point of program execution. It is responsible for the high-level organization of the program's functionality, and typically has access to the command arguments given to the program when it is executed.

When the execution of program begins, the system calls the "main" function, which marks the entry point of the program. Every program must have one function named "main" with following constraints:

- No other function in the program can be named "main".
- "main" function cannot be defined as inline or static.
- "main" function cannot be called from within a program.
- The address of "main" function cannot be taken.
- "main" function cannot be overloaded.

Following are the prototype of the "main" function:

- int main(void)
- int main()
- int main(int argc, char **argv)
- int main(int argc, char *argv[])

4.4.1 Main Function with argv, argc[]

argc and argv are referred to the names given to the parameters to the function. The first parameter, argc (argument count) is an integer that indicates how many arguments were entered on the command line when the program was started. The second parameter, argv (argument vector), is an array of pointers to arrays of character objects.

The first element of the array, argv[0], is a pointer to the character array that contains the name of the program that is being run from the command line. argv[1] indicates the first argument passed to the program, argv[2] the second argument, and so on.

4.5 Testing and Debugging

Testing and debugging are important steps in program development. Both testing and debugging deal with program errors and make program free from errors, whereas they are used for the separate mean.

4.5.1 Debugging

Debugging is the process of detecting syntactical errors in the program. Errors of the programs are also known as "bug". Debugging can be performed during the execution of program. During debugging of the program, programmer can execute the code line by line. The process of debugging help programmer to examine the operation on value of variable or the value passes to function during line by line execution of program. Debuggers are a software tool which allows the programmer to monitor the execution of a program, stop it, restart it, and set breakpoints during execution.

4.5.2 Testing

Testing is the process of validating the precision of the program. The process of testing begins after the development of program. Testing is intended to making surety that the program is free from all types of syntactical and logical errors and is ready to use. The criteria and heuristics of testing can be defined before the coding of program begins. When the program is coded completely the testing is performed according to defined criteria or heuristics. Following are the types of software testing

- **Black box testing** – In this type of testing internal system design is not considered in this type of testing. Tests are based on requirements and functionality.
- **White box testing** – This testing is based on knowledge of the internal logic of an application's code. Also known as Glass box Testing. Internal software and code working should be known for this type of testing. Tests are based on coverage of code statements, branches, paths, conditions.
- **Unit testing** – Testing of individual software components or modules. Typically done by the programmer and not by testers, as it requires detailed knowledge of the internal program design and code. may require developing test driver modules or test harnesses.
- **Functional testing** – This type of testing ignores the internal parts and focus on the output is as per requirement or not. Black-box type testing geared to functional requirements of an application.

- **System testing** – Entire system is tested as per the requirements. Black-box type testing that is based on overall requirements specifications, covers all combined parts of a system.
- **Acceptance testing** -Normally this type of testing is done to verify if system meets the customer specified requirements. User or customer do this testing to determine whether to accept application.
- **Performance testing** – Term often used interchangeably with 'stress' and 'load' testing. To check whether system meets performance requirements. Used different performance and load tools to do this.
- **Usability testing** – User-friendliness check. Application flow is tested, Can new user understand the application easily, Proper help documented whenever user stuck at any point. Basically system navigation is checked in this testing.
- **Recovery testing** – Testing how well a system recovers from crashes, hardware failures, or other catastrophic problems.
- **Security testing** – Can system be penetrated by any hacking way. Testing how well the system protects against unauthorized internal or external access. Checked if system, database is safe from external attacks.
- **Comparison testing** – Comparison of product strengths and weaknesses with previous versions or other similar products.
- **Alpha testing** – In house virtual user environment can be created for this type of testing. Testing is done at the end of development. Still minor design changes may be made as a result of such testing.
- **Beta testing** – Testing typically done by end-users or others. Final testing before releasing application for commercial purpose.

Multiple Choice Questions

1. The expressions written in the 'for' loop, are separated using a _____.

   A) colon
   B) comma
   C) semicolon
   D) hyphen

2. The condition being tested within the _____ control structure may use relational or

   logical operations.

   A) while
   B) switch
   C) break
   D) continue

3. 'continue' statement is used to
   A) go to the next iteration in a loop
   B) come out of a loop
   C) exit and return to the main function
   D) restarts iterations from beginning of loop
4. Which among the following is a unconditional control structure ?
   A) do-while   B) if-else
   C) goto   D) for
5. A "do... while " loop terminates, when the expression written in ` while ` returns _____
   A) 1   B) 0
   C) -1   D) NULL
6. The body of a ` WHILE ` Loop has
   A) one statement only   B) atleast two statements
   C) one or more statements D) None of above.
7. Which is not conditional and unconditional branching ?
   A) if   B) switch
   C) break   D) include
8. Which of the following statement about pre -test loops are true?
   A) If a pre-test loop limit test is false ,the loop executes one more time
   B) Pre-test loop initialization is done first in the loop body
   C) Pre-test loops execute a minimum of one time
   D) The update for a pre-test loop must be a part of the loop body
9. A switch statement is used to
   A) switch between functions
   B) switch from one variable to another
   C) to choose from multiple possibilities
   D) to use switching variables
10. What is the meaning of 'while (1)'?
    A) Execution of loop only once
    B) Execution of loop at least once
    C) Infinite Loop
    D) No execution of the loop

11. Find the correct form of ` nested if `
    A) if(if(condition)) do this;
    B) else(if(condition) do this;
    C) if(condition) { if(condition) do this; }
    D) if&&if(condition)
12. Find out the wrong statement
    A) if(condition) do this;
    B) if(condition) { do this; and this; }
    C) else do this;
    D) if(condition) do this; else do this;
13. Which symbol is used to separate multiple initialization in the 'for' loop?
    A) &&
    B) ,
    C) ;
    D) None of the above
14. The keyword ………….. allows to take the control to the beginning of the loop, by passing the statements inside the loop, which have not yet been executed.
    A) goto
    B) for
    C) continue
    D) case
15. Which of the following loop is not used in ` C ` language?
    A) 'for' loop
    B) 'if...else'
    C) 'Repeat...until' loop
    D) 'do..while' loop
16. Which of the following ` for ` statements is wrong?
    A) for(i=0, j=1;i<5;i++)
    B) for(i=0;i<5;i++);
    C) for(i=0,i<5,i++)
    D) for(;i>7;)
17. How many ` ; ` (semicolon) are included in 'for' statement (or loop)?
    A) 0
    B) 1
    C) 2
    D) 3
18. The _____statement allows the programmer to take the control to the beginning of the loop, bypassing the statement inside the loop which has not yet been executed.
    A) while
    B) continue
    C) go to
    D) if
19. The _____loop allows programmer to specify three things about a loop in single line.
    A) for
    B) while
    C) goto
    D) switch
20. Which of the following statements about the ` switch ` statement is false?
    A) No two case labels can have the same value
    B) The switch control expression must be of 'character' type
    C) The case-labled constant can be a constant or a variable
    D) Two case labels can be associated with the same statement series

21. A two way selection is implemented in the program, by using _____ statement.
    A) case   B) else..if   C) switch   D) if..else
22. A 'do...while' loop is useful when we want that statement within the loop must be executed_____.
    A) only once
    B) at least once
    C) more than once
    D) none of above.
23. The _____ logic is used to produce loops in program, depending on some condition.
    A) Iteration logic
    B) Selection logic
    C) Sequence logic
    D. Decision logic
24. What is a function parameter?
    A) A constant
    B) A variable
    C) A function
    D) all of these
25. Following are the not looping statements.
    A) if-then-else
    B) do-while
    C) while
    D) for loop
26. When we pass an array of a structure to a function it is passed by the_____ mechanism.
    A) Call by value
    B) Call by reference
    C) Call by name
    D) None
27. In the following 'C' program, find out the error in the 'while' loop, if any?
    main( )
    {
        int i=1;
        while()
        {
        printf("%d",i++);
        if(i>10)
        break;
    } }
    A) The condition in the while loop is must
    B) There should be at least a semicolon in the while( )
    C) The while loop should be replaced by for loop
    D) No error

28. Can we use logical operators in ` if-else ` statement?
   A) yes   B) no   C) error   D) Both B and C

29. Which of following statements about ` for ` loop are correct?
   A) Index value is retained outside the loop
   B) Index value can be changed from within the loop
   C) Goto can be jump, out of the loop
   D) All of above

30. The control statement that allows us to make a decision from number of choices is called _____ .
   A) structure   B) switch statement
   C) if loop   D) for loop

31. The 'break' statement is used to exit from _____ .
   A) an ' if ' statement   B) a for loop
   C) a program   D) the main ( ) function

32. With which of the following arguments, the main function is called ?
   A) argc   B) argv
   C) None of these   D) both a & b

33. Which of the following is the correct syntax of for loop?
   A) for (initialization, condition, inc/ dec)
   B) for (initialization, condition, inc/dec) { { ------; ------; ------; ------; } }
   C) for (initialization; condition; inc/dec)
   D) None of these { ------; ------; }

34. How many post test loops are present in C?
   A) One   B) Two   C) Three   D) None of these

35. How many loops are present in C?
   A) One   B) Two   C) Three   D) None of these

36. Which of the following is false statement for ` C ` ?
   A) A keyword can be used as a variables name
   B) variable names can contain digits
   C) variable name do not contain blank space
   D) capital letters can be used in variables names

37. Which loop doesn't require to write ` ; ` after the loop condition?
   A) while   B) do...while   C) for   D) none

38. When a function is calling itself again and again it is called as ----------
    A) Loop B) Interaction C) Recursion D) Repitition
39. Even though the condition is wrong the do while loop executes at least one time -------
    A) Twice B) Once C) Thrice D) Will not execute
40. Which of the following is iterative control structures?
    A) if statement
    B) if-else statement
    C) do-while loop
    D) goto statement
41. Which of the following control structures are used in an iteration logic _____.
    A) IF....THEN & IF...THEN...ELSE
    B) DO ..& WHILE
    C) DO..WHILE & REPEAT...UNTILL
    D) DO..WHILE & IF...ELSE
42. In a while loop the parantheses after the 'while' contains a _____
    A) condition B) statement C) count D) value
43. `If-else` statement is used as _____.
    A) Decision control structure
    B) Conditional statements
    C) Repetition of code
    D) Both B and C
44. A _____ statement causes the program control to end up almost anywhere in the program.
    A) go to B) for C) while D) do....while
45. Which of the following statement is correct related to an if-else statement ?
    A) If we use an if it is compulsory to use an else
    B) Every if-else can be replaced by ? : operator.
    C) Nested if-else is allowed.
    D) Only one if-else can be written.
46. The Maximum number of arguments that a function can take is ?
    A) 10 B) 2 C) 4 D) None of above
47. Which is the correct syntax of do while loop?
    A) do { ------; ------;   )
    B) do{ ------; ------;   )
    C) do { while (condition) ------; ------;
    D) None of these

48. Syntax of while loop is _____.
   A) while { (condition); ------; ------;
   B) while(condition) { ------; ------; }
   C) while {-----; ------; }(condition);
   D) none of these

49. Loop inside another loop is called as_____
   A) Integrated Loop   B) Nested Loop
   C) Control Loop   D) Loop

50. Which of the following is not a control statement in C?
   A) for   B. while   C. do-while   D. else

51. When an `if..else` statement is included within an `if..else` statement, it is known as a _____.
   A) Next if statement   B) another if statement
   C) combined if statement   D) Nested if statement

52. A `goto` statement is_____.
   A) Conditional transfer of control to another statement.
   B) Unconditional transfer of control to another statement
   C) Equivalent to break statement
   D) Equivalent to continue statement

53. Which of the following is an iterative control structure?
   A) If   B) if else   C) do while   D) go to

54. point out the error, if any, in the `for` loop?
   ```
   #include<stdio.h>
   main()
   {
       int i=1;
       for(;;)
       { printf("%d", i++);
       if(i>10)
       break;
       }
   }
   ```

A) The condition in the for loop is a must
B) The two semicolons should be dropped
C) The for loop should be replaced by while loop
D) No Error

55. A ` while ` loop is knowm as a
A) exit controlled loop
B) entry controlled loop
C) exit controlled loop
D) none of the above

56. A ` do-while ` loop is useful when the statements within the loop must be executed:
A) Only once
B) At least once
C) More than once
D) None of the above

57. A case in ` switch ` statement is terminated by _____ if control should not fall through the successive cases.
A) break
B) break;
C) ;
D) break,

58. The break statement is used to exit from?
A) an 'if' statement
B) 'for' statement
C) Both from the 'if' and 'for' statement
D) the main function

59. Which of the following is not infinite loop?
A) int i=1; while(1){i++;}
B) for(; ;);
C) int True=0, false; while(True) { False=1;}
D) int I;for(i=0;1<10;i++);

60. In what sequence the initialization, testing and execution of the body is done in a ` do-while ` loop
A) initialization, execution of the body, testing
B) Execution of the body, initialization, testing
C) nitialization, testing, execution of the body
D) None of the above

61. Difference between ` while ` and ` do-while `
    A) 'while' loop executes one or more times and 'do-while' executes zero or more times
    B) Both 'while' loop and 'do-while' executes one or more times
    C) Both 'while' loop and 'do-while' executes zero or more times
    D) 'while' loop executes zero or more times and 'do-while' executes one or more times

62. Which statement is used to terminate the current loop
    A) exit
    B) break
    C) Both exit and break
    D) None of above

63. Which of the following operator is used to write expressions in ` C ` ?
    A) { }
    B) ( )
    C) [ ]
    D) None of the above

64. The general form of ` for ` statement in C is
    A) for(initialise counter, test counter, increment counter)
    B) for(increment counter; initialise counter; test counter)
    C) for(test counter; increment counter; initialise counter);
    D) for(initialise counter; test counter; increment counter)

65. The if statement in ` C ` is terminated by
    A) {
    B) :
    C) ,
    D) None of the above

66. The Correct syntax for the ` for ` loop in ` C ` is _____.
    A) for(i=1; i<=MAX ; i++)
    B) for(i=1: i<=MAX: i++)
    C) for(i=1, i<=MAX , i++);
    D) None of the above

67. Which one of the following is the correct syntax for printing the octal value of integer 'a' to the console?
    A) printf("%f",a);
    B) printf("%d",a);
    C) printf("%o",a);
    D) printf("%x",a)

68. Which of the following data types is not valid in a switch .. case statement?
    A) character
    B) integer
    C) enum
    D) float

69. In the program given below, point out the error, if any, in the while loop else predict the correct answer?

```
main()
{
    void fun();
    int i=1;
    while(i<=5)
    {
    printf("%d",i);
    if(i>2) goto here;
    }
}
void fun()
```
A) Syntax Error : Undefined label 'here'
B) it works
C) 1 1 1 1 1
D) 1 1

70. Which among the following is a unconditional control structure?
    A) do-while   B) if-else   C) goto   D) for

71. A 'continue' statement terminates a_____.
    A) function   B) iteration
    C) body of a loop   D) None of the above

72. A 'switch' statement is used to make a decision _____.
    A) to switch the processor to execute some
    B) between two alternatives
    C) amongst many alternatives
    D) none of these

73. 'break' statement is used for_____.
    A) terminating a loop   B) continuing a loop
    C) exiting from a program   D) all of the above

74. The _____statement is used in 'C' to branch unconditionally from one point to another in the program.
    A) if   B) for   C) while   D) goto

75. Which of the ` C ` loops check the condition before a loop is executed?
    A) while   B) for
    C) both a & b   D) d0 ---while

76. A function gets called when the function name is followed by the optional arguments and a _____
    A) colon   B) semicolon   C) hyphen   D) bracket
77. A _____ is a self contained block of statements that performs a coherent task of some kind.
    A) function   B) compiler
    C) statement   D) body of program
78. A _____ statement is very useful while writing the menu driven programs.
    A) while   B) break   C) switch   D) if
79. The three parts of the loop expression in the 'for' loop are- the _____expression; the_____expression; the_____expression
    A) Testing,Initialization,Termination. B) Termination,Testing,Initiation
    C) Initiation; Testing; Termination D) None of these
80. Is Nesting of if-else statements is possible ?
    A) Yes   B) NO   C) Can't say   D) None of these
81. A 'do-while' loop is useful when we want that the statements within the loop must be executed:
    A) Only once   B) At least once
    C) More then ones   D) None of the above
82. Which loop is a pre-test loop?
    A) for   B) do-while   C) while   D) a and c
83. In "do-while" loop if while condition is found to be false _____ .
    A) the loop will be continued
    B) the loop will be terminated and program will be halted
    C) the loop will be terminated
    D) None of above
84. In "if-else" logic _____ .
    A) every "if" condition will be followed by an "else".
    B) some of the "else" may not have "if" preceeding it
    C) closing "if-else" block occurs at "else" only.
    D) None of above
85. break statement can be simulated by using
    A) goto   B) return
    C) exit   D) any of the above features

86. In switch case construct, case values works only with (i) integer constant (ii) floting point constant (iii) variables (iv) character constant
   A) all are correct
   B) option (I) are correct
   C) option (ii) is correct
   D) options (i),(iii),(iv) are correct

87. In a ` for ` loop more than one initialization or loop expressions are separated using a _____.
   A) ;
   B) ,
   C) blank
   D) tab

88. How many iterations will be there for the following ` while ` loop?
 main()
 {
 int I=0;
 int NUM =10;
 while(I < NUM)
 {
 I=I+2;
 I=I-1;
 }
 }
   A) 9
   B) 10
   C) 11
   D) 12

89. If a ` while ` loop condition is checked for the seventh time, then the loop has already executed for _____ times.
   A) 0
   B) 5
   C) 6
   D) 7

90. In a ` for ` loop how many semicolons are allowed?
   A) greater than or equal to 2
   B) exactly two
   C) 0,1 or 2
   D) any number

91. Which statement can stop a loop?
   A) continue
   B) break
   C) initialization
   D) if

92. Missing condition in while loop will generate a _____.
   A) compiler error
   B) runtime error
   C) warning
   D) infinite loop

93. Missing condition in while loop will generate a _____.
   A) compiler error
   B) runtime error
   C) warning
   D) infinite loop

94. Which loops are similar in the behavior?
   A) for & do..while
   B) while & do..while
   C) while & for
   D) do..while, for & while

95. In a worst case how many times a 'while' loop executes?
   A) 0
   B) 1
   C) n times
   D) infinite

96. During use of nested ` if……else ` the dangling else problem encountered when _____
   A) a matching else is not available for an if.
   B) a matching else is available for an if.
   C) a matching if is not available for an else.
   D) a matching if is available for an else.

97. Which of the following is right syntax for 'do-while' in 'C' language?
    A) do{while};
    B) do{..}while(condition);
    C) do{condition}while
    D) do{while}condition;

98. Which of the following is right syntax for 'while' in 'C' language.?
    A) while(condition)
    B) while(condition);
    C) condition(while);
    D) {while}(condition);

99. In "do- while" loop, the body of the loop will get executed even though while condition false
    A) only once
    B) At least once
    C) More than once
    D) None of these

100. Which of the ` C ` loop is a pretest loop
    A) Do... while
    B) For
    C) While
    D) Both for and while

101. A 'goto' statement is
    A) Conditional transfer of control to another statement
    B) Unconditional transfer of control to another statement
    C) Equivalent to break statement
    D) Equivalent to continue statement0

102. A 'Go to' statement
    A) Jumps directly to the label name
    B) Executes the statements in the sequence till the label name is found
    C) Performs no action
    D) None of the above

103. Which loop allows to omit the 'condition' part?
    A) while   B) do...while   C) for   D) none

104. Which part of a 'loop' allows the control to flow inside or outside the ` loop ` ?
    A) loop statement
    B) loop expression
    C) loop condition
    D) initialization

105. Which of the following is not a 'loop' construct in 'C' ?
    A) for   B) while   C) repeat until   D) do while

106. Which amongst the following keywords is not at all required while writing a basic 'switch – case' construct?
    A) default   B) case   C) break   D) continue

107. Which combinations of writing 'if..else' and 'switch' statements inside a program is possible?
    A) writing switch in if else
    B) writing if else in switch
    C) writing one switch in another
    D) all of above

108. The 'continue' statement cannot be used with
    A) for   B) switch   C) do   D) while

109. A Debugger is_____
    A) a compiler
    B) an active debugger
    C) a C interpreter
    D) a analyzing tool in C

110. Which of the following are the parameter passing methods
 1.pass by value.
 2. pass by reference
 3. pass by address?
    A) Flowchart
    B) Pseudo code
    C) Structure chart
    D) Program Map

111. Which of the following statements about the 'do...while' loop is false?
    A) A 'do..while' loop executes one or more iterations
    B) Any statement may be used as the action in a 'do..while'
    C) The 'do..while' is the only loop that requires a semicolon.
    D) The limit test in a 'do..while' loop is executed at the beginning of each iteration

112. Which of the following is not a iterative construct?
    A) a for loop
    B) a do-while loop
    C) an if-else statement
    D) a while loop

113. Debugging can be done only _____
    A) only after the program is coded
    B) before the program coding
    C) after the main statement
    D) None of these

114. Debugger are the software tools which enable the programmer to _____
    A) monitor the execution of a program
    B) stop it and restart it
    C) change values in the memory
    D) All of the above

115. 1) Manual execution, 2) Printing the intermediate results in the prgram , 3) Debugger are the methods used to locate and correct _____
    A) Logical errors
    B) Compile-time errors
    C) Run-time errors
    D) Syntax errors

116. Testing furnishes a criticism or comparison that compares the state and behavior of the product against a _____
    A) Specification   B) Verification
    C) Validation   D) None of these

117. In _____ testing we acutally run the program with a given set of test cases in a given development stage .
    A) Dynamic   B) Static   C) Black box   D) White box

118. Verification process ensures that the product that has been built matches all the _____
    A) Validations
    B) Customer requirments
    C) Specifications
    D) Documents

119. The process involves ensuring that the final product matches the customer requirments is called as _____
    A) Verification   B) Static testing
    C) Validation   D) Dynamic testing

120. Detailed understandind of the internal behavior of the product is not required in _____
    A) Unit testing   B) Black box testing
    C) White box testing D) System testing

121. Tester can simply verify the fact that for a given input value, the output value, is the same as the expected value specified in the test case using _____
    A) Black box testing B) White box testing
    C) Integration testing D) Unit testing

122. To perform white box testing the tester must have access to _____
    A) internal data structures   B) code
    C) algorithms   D) All of the above

123. White box testing includes all _____
    A) Dynamic testing   B) Static testing
    C) Black box testing D) None of these

124. Unit testing tests the _____
    A) Complete software B) Module
    C) Algorithm   D) Data structures

125. In unit testing each _____ of the software is tested to verify that the detailed design for the unit has been correctly implemented.
    A) Unit   B) Code   C) Module   D) Algorithm

126. Integration testing exposes defects in the interfaces and interaction between _____
    A) A single module   B) Modules
    C) Data structures   D) Algorithm

127. _____ testing tests the minimal software component or module.
    A) Integraton   B) System I
    C) Unit   D) System integration

128. _____ testing exposes defects in the interfaces and interaction between integrated components.
    A) Unit   B) Integration
    C) System integration   D) System

129. System testing tests a completely integrated system to verify that it meets its _____
    A) Requirments   B) Specification
    C) Validation   D) Verification

130. _____ testing tests a completely integrated system to verify that it meets its requirments.
    A) Unit   B) System
    C) System integration   D) Integration

131. _____ testing verifies that a system is integrated to an external or third party systems defined in the systen requirments.
    A) System integration   B) System
    C) Unit   D) Integration

132. System integration testing verifies that a _____ is integrated to external or third party systems defined in the system requirments.
    A) Unit   B) System   C) Data structures   D) Algorithm

133. _____ is not the testing method.
    A) Black box   B) White box
    C) Red box   D) Unit

134. Software testing is used in association with the _____ & _____ .
    A) Verification & Validation   B) Static & Dynamic Testing
    C) Black box & White box testing   D) None of these

Unit 4 | 4.31

135. Unit, Integration, System & System integration are the _____ methods.
    A) Debugging B) Testing C) Programming D) All of these

136. Testing is a____if a program does not work correctly
    A) Failure B) Success C) Complete D) Partial

137. The process of collecting, organizing & maintaining a complete record of development of programs is called as _____.
    A) Testing
    B) Documentation
    C) Debugging
    D) Coding

138. Debugging is done by_____
    A) Compiler B) Programmer C) Editor D) None of above

139. Black box testing is of the following form:
    A) Test engineer has no knowledge of the code and does not know how the code functions, and testing is based mostly on requirement sheets.
    B) Test engineer has partial knowledge of the code but no knowledge about functionality of the code.
    C) Test engineer has no knowledge of the code, but has full awareness of the functionality of the code.
    D) Test engineer has complete awareness of the code and functionality of the program and testing is based on both

140. White box testing is of the following form:
    A) Test engineer has complete knowledge of the code and functionality of the program, and testing is based on this knowledge.
    B) Test engineer has no knowledge of the code but has full knowledge of the functionality of the program.
    C) Test engineer has complete knowledge of the code but has no knowledge of the functionality of the program.
    D) Test engineer has no knowledge of the code and does not know how the code functions, and testing is based mostly on requirement sheets.

141. What is meant by "Program Testing"?
    A) process of eliminating program errors
    B) process of validating correctness of program.
    C) prosess of writing program
    D) process of running program

FPL – I ENGG. (F.E. SEM. I) C PROGRAMMING

142. Testing is successful when
   A) Desired output has been obtained
   B) Syntax errors are removed
   C) All errors are removed
   D) Logical errors are removed

143. Loops are called
   A) Sequential logic structures
   B) Decision logic structures
   C) Iterative logic structures
   D) None of the above

144. 'IF...THEN...ELSE' structure is called
   A) Selection logic structures
   B) Sequence logic structures
   C) Iteration logic structures
   D) Program logic structures

Answers

1.	C	2.	A	3.	A	4.	C	5.	B
6.	C	7.	D	8.	D	9.	C	10.	C
11.	C	12.	C	13.	B	14.	C	15.	C
16.	C	17.	C	18.	B	19.	A	20.	B
21.	B	22.	B	23.	A	24.	B	25.	A
26.	B	27.	A	28.	A	29.	D	30.	B
31.	B	32.	D	33.	C	34.	A	35.	C
36.	A	37.	A	38.	C	39.	B	40.	C
41.	C	42.	A	43.	A	44.	A	45.	C
46.	D	47.	D	48.	B	49.	B	50.	D
51.	D	52.	B	53.	C	54.	D	55.	B
56.	B	57.	B	58.	C	59.	C	60.	A
61.	D	62.	B	63.	B	64.	D	65.	D
66.	A	67.	C	68.	D	69.	A	70.	C
71.	B	72.	C	73.	A	74.	D	75.	C
76.	B	77.	A	78.	C	79.	C	80.	A
81.	B	82.	D	83.	C	84.	D	85.	A

86.	D	87.	B	88.	B	89.	C	90.	B
91.	B	92.	A	93.	D	94.	C	95.	A
96.	A	97.	B	98.	A	99.	B	100.	D
101.	B	102.	A	103.	C	104.	C	105.	C
106.	D	107.	D	108.	B	109.	D	110.	B
111.	D	112.	C	113.	A	114.	D	115.	A
116.	A	117.	A	118.	C	119.	C	120.	B
121.	A	122.	D	123.	B	124.	B	125.	A
126.	B	127.	C	128.	B	129.	A	130.	B
131.	A	132.	B	133.	C	134.	A	135.	B
136.	A	137.	B	138.	B	139.	A	140.	A
141.	B	142.	A	143.	C	144.	A		

LABORATORY ASSIGNMENTS

Group A. Assignments

1. **Write a program in (Eclipse) C++ to display string "Hello World!".**

Program .

Use and Study of Linux GUI and Commands.

Theory: Companies such as RedHat, SuSE and Mandriva have sprung up, providing packaged Linux distributions suitable for mass consumption. They integrated a great deal of graphical user interfaces (GUIs), developed by the community, in order to ease management of programs and services.

Linux Pros/advantages

1. Linux is free open source operating system.
2. It is portable to any hardware platform:
3. It was made to keep on running
4. It is secure and versatile:
5. It is scalable:
6. The Linux OS and quite some Linux applications have very short debug-times:

Linux Cons/Disadvantages

1. There are far too many different distributions:
2. Linux is not very user friendly and confusing for beginners:

Linux Commands

1. **ls - Short listing of directory contents**

   ls -laxo

   ls command, which lists files with permissions, shows hidden files, displays in a column format, and doesn't show the group.

2. **cd - change directories**

   Use cd to change directories. Type cd followed by the name of a directory to access that directory. Keep in mind that you are always in a directory and can navigate to directories hierarchically above or below.

3. **mv- change the name of a directory**

   Type mv followed by the current name of a directory and the new name of the directory.

4. pwd - print working directory

will show you the full path to the directory you are currently in. This is very handy to use, especially when performing some of the other commands on this page

5. rmdir - Remove an existing directory

Removes directories and files within the directories recursively.

Change User Commands

1. **useradd** - Adding a new user
   - **-d** home directory
   - **-s** starting program (shell)
   - **-p** password
   - **-g** (primary group assigned to the users)
   - **-G** (Other groups the user belongs to)
   - **-m** (Create the user's home directory

2. **usermod** - Modifying existing user
   - **-d** home directory
   - **-s** starting program (shell)
   - **-p** password
   - **-g** (primary group assigned to the users)
   - **-G** (Other groups the user belongs to)

3. **userdel** - Deleting a user
   - **-r** (remove home directory)

4. **passwd** - User's Password
   - **user's name** (Only required if you are root and want to change another user's password)

5. - **Switch User**
   - To switch to another user, use the **su** command. This is most commonly used to switch to the root account.

privileges commands

The second method of changing permissions is using the symbolic mode. The generalformat for the symbolic mode is:

who <operator> permission

1. **who** - who specifies which permission group we are changing. Possible values are:
   - **u** - user's permissions
   - **g** - group's permissions
   - **o** - other's permissions
   - **a** - all permissions (user, group, and other)
2. **operator** - specifies which action to take. Possible values are:
   - **+** - Adds the permission
   - **-** - Removes the permission
   - **=** - Sets the permission exactly
3. **permissions** - specifies which permission bit to change. The ones we are concerned with are:
   - **r** - the read bit
   - **w** - the write bit
   - **x** - the execute bit
4. **tty Command**

   Writes to standard output the full path name of your terminal.

   Syntax: /usr/bin/tty [-s]

   The **tty** command writes the name of your terminal to standard output. If your standard input is not a terminal and you do not specify the **-s** flag, you get the message Standard input is not a tty.

5. **make** - GNU make utility to maintain groups of programs

   make [**-f** *makefile*] [option] ... target ...

   The purpose of the *make* utility is to determine automatically which pieces of a large program need to be recompiled, and issue the commands to recompile them.

6. **sudo** - execute a command as another user

   sudo -V | -h | -l | -L | -v | -k | -K | -s | [-H] [-P] [-S] [-b] |

   [**-p** *prompt*] [**-c** *class*|-] [**-a** *auth_type*] [**-u** *username*|#*uid*] command

   sudo allows a permitted user to execute a *command* as the superuser or another user, as specified in the *sudoers* file. The real and effective uid and gid are set to match those of the target user as specified in the passwd file

yum command

yum list updates: Display list of updated software

yum update: Patch up system by applying all updates

rpm -qa

yum list installed: List all installed packages

2. Handling and Use of Eclipse Editor for Creating Projects in C, python(Pydev), Java.

Theory: Eclipse as an integrated development environment (IDE) for Java. Eclipse is created by an Open Source community and is used in several different areas, e.g. as a development environment for Java or Android applications. The Eclipse IDE can be extended with additional software components. Eclipse calls these software components *plug-ins*. It is also possible to use Eclipse as a basis for creating general purpose applications.

2.1. Starting Eclipse :

To start Eclipse double-click on the file eclipse.exe (Microsoft Windows) or eclipse (Linux / Mac) in the directory where you unpacked Eclipse.

The system will prompt you for a *workspace*. The *workspace* is the place in which you work. Select an empty directory and press the OK button.

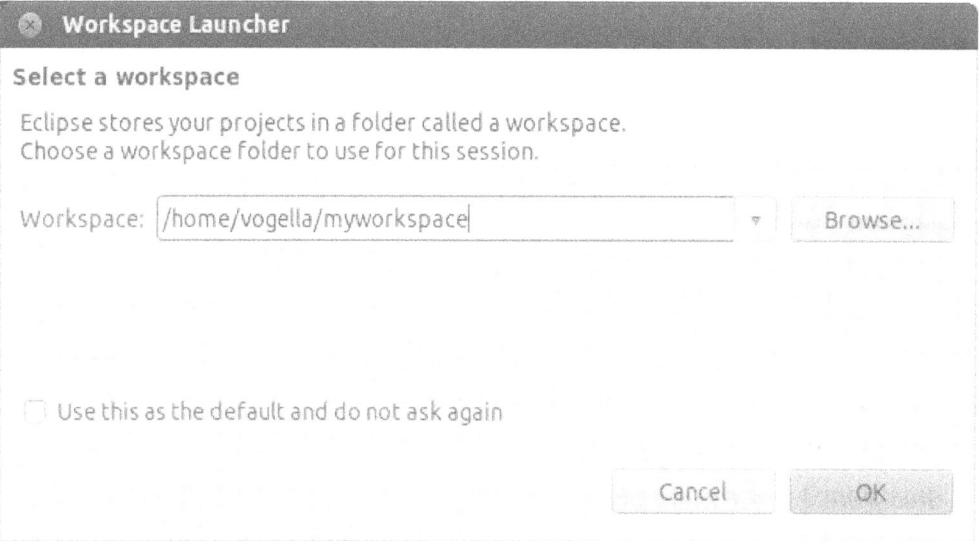

Eclipse will start and show the Welcome page. Close the welcome page by pressing the X beside Welcome.

FPL – I ENGG. (F.E. SEM. I)   ASSIGNMENTS

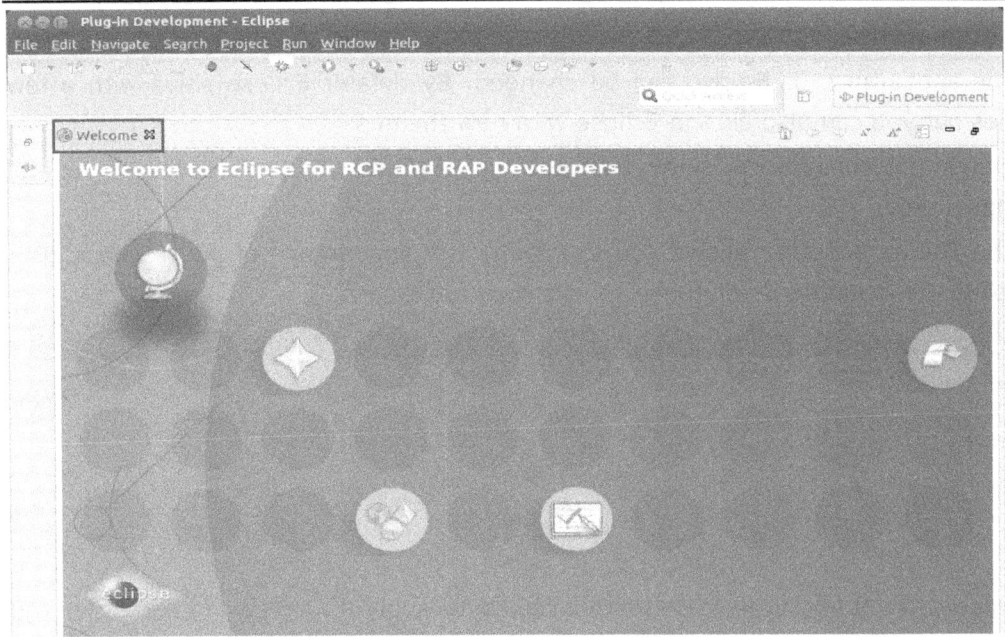

After you closed the welcome screen you should see a screen similar to the following.

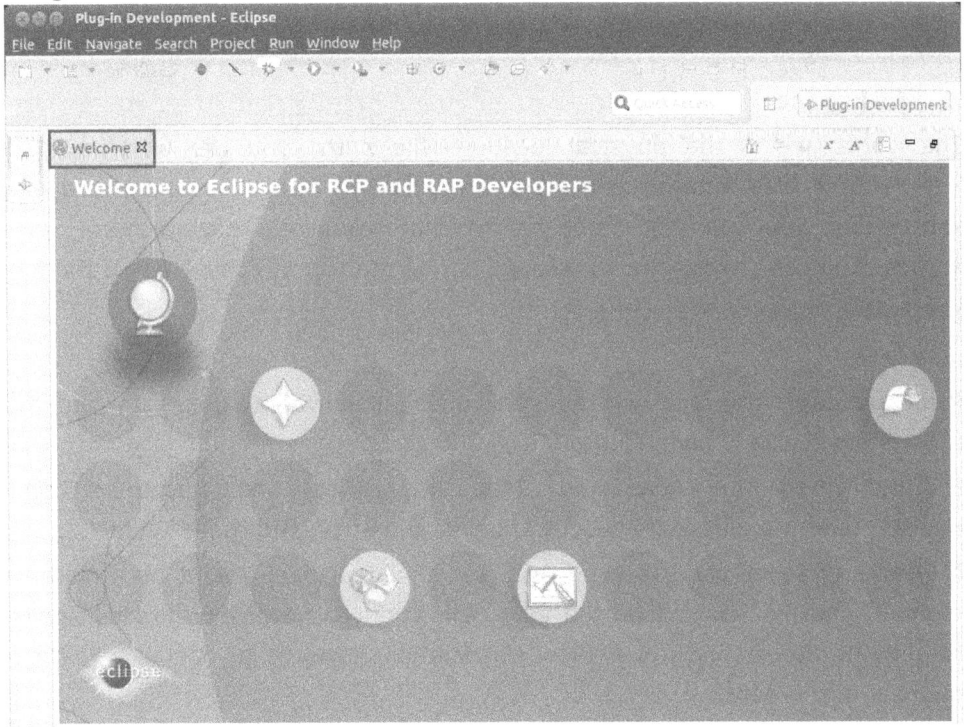

2.2. Appearance:

The appearance of Eclipse can be changed. By default Eclipse ships with a few themes but you can also extend Eclipse with new themes.

To change the appearance, select from the menu Window → Preferences → General → Appearance.

The Theme selection allows you to change the appearance of your Eclipse IDE. Disabling the animations will make your Eclipse run faster.

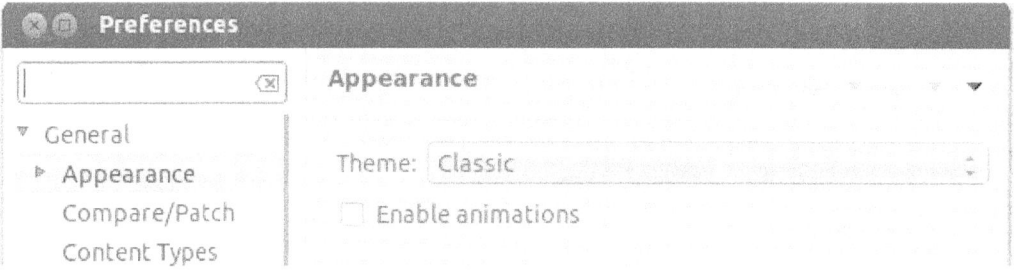

Please note that you need to restart Eclipse to apply a new styling correctly. You can also install new themes.

2.3 Eclipse user interface overview

Eclipse provides *Perspectives*, *Views* and *Editors*. *Views* and *Editors* are grouped into *Perspectives*.

2.3.1. Workspace

The *workspace* is the physical location (file path) you are working in. Your projects, source files, images and other artifacts can be stored and saved in your workspace but you can also refer to external resources, e.g. projects, in your *workspace*. You can choose the workspace during startup of Eclipse or via the menu (File → Switch Workspace → Others).

2.3.2. Parts

Parts are user interface components which allow you to navigate and modify data. *Parts* are typically divided into *Views* and *Editors*.

The distinction into *Views* and *Editors* is primarily not based on technical differences, but on a different concept of using and arranging these *Parts*.

A *View* is typically used to work on a set of data, which might be a hierarchical structure. If data is changed via the *View*, this change is typically directly applied to the underlying data structure. A *View* sometimes allows us to open an *Editor* for a selected set of the data.

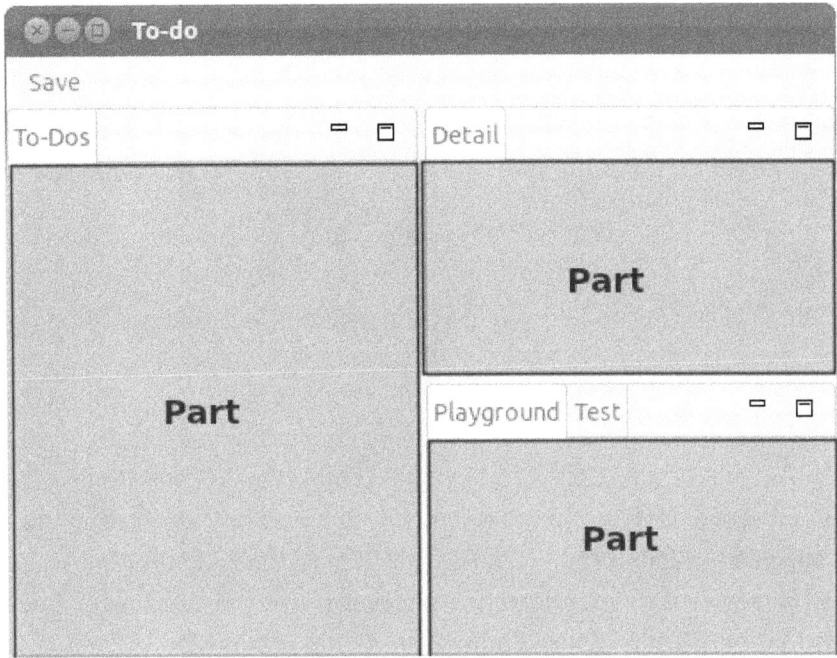

An example for a *View* is the *Java Package Explorer*, which allow you browse the files of Eclipse Projects. If you choose to change data in the Package Explorer, e.g. if you rename a file, the file name is directly changed on the file system.

Editors are typically used to modify a single data element, e.g. a file or a data object. To apply the changes made in an editor to the data structure, the user has to explicitly save the editor content.

Editors were traditionally placed in a certain area, called the *editor area*. Until Eclipse 4 this was a hard limitation, it was not possible to move an *Editor* out of this area; Eclipse 4 allows the user to place *Editors* at any position in a *Perspective* or even outside a *Perspective*.

For example the Java Editor is used to modify Java source files. Changes to the source file are applied once the user selects the *Save* command.

2.3.3. Perspective

A *Perspective* is a visual container for a set of *Parts*. The Eclipse IDE uses *Perspectives* to arrange *Parts* for different development tasks. You can switch *Perspectives* in your Eclipse IDE via the

Window → Open Perspective → Other menu entry.

The main perspectives used in the Eclipse IDE are Java perspective for Java development and the Debug perspective for debugging Java applications.

You can change the layout and content within a *Perspective* by opening or closing *Parts* and by re-arranging them.

To open a new *Part* in your current *Perspective* use the Window → Show View → Other menu entry. The following Show View dialog allows you to search for certain Parts.

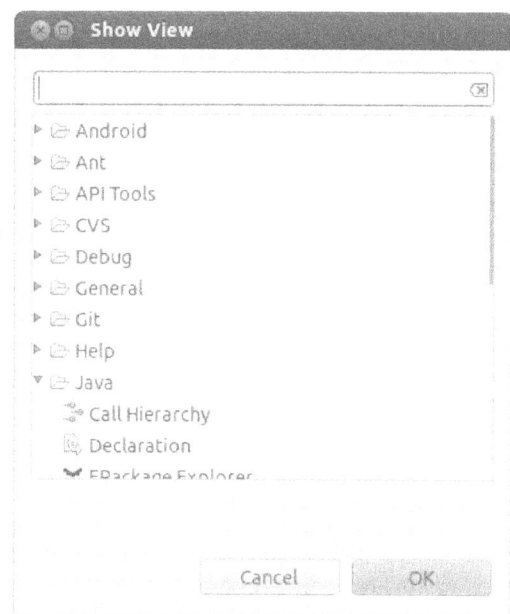

In cases you want to reset your current perspective to its default, you can use the Window → Reset Perspective menu entry.

You can save your *Perspective* via Window → Save Perspective As....

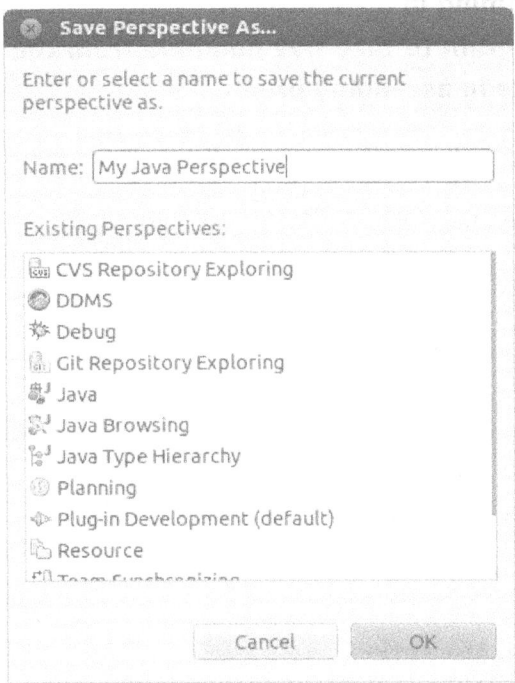

---

3. **Using Eclipse to write/Test "Hello! World" Program in C.**

Program:

```
#include stdio
Using namespace std
void main()
{
    printf(" Hello");
}
```

OUTPUT

Hello

FPL – I ENGG. (F.E. SEM. I)   ASSIGNMENTS

Group B. Assignments

Foundation Programming in C (Atleast 8)

   4. Write a C program to take five numbers from the console and display them back to console in ascending order.

Program:

```c
#include<stdio.h>
#include<conio.h>
void main()
{
    int num[20],m,p,i,j,temp;
    clrscr();
    printf("\nEnter  the 5 number:");
    for( m=0; m<5; m++)
     scanf("%d",&num[m]);
    for(i=0;i<5;i++)
    {
       for(j=i+1;j<5;j++)
          {
          if(num[i]>num[j])

          temp=num[i];
          num[i]=num[j];
          num[j]=temp;

          }
    }
printf("\nNumbers in ascending order:");
    for(j=0; j<5; j++)
    {
    printf("%d\t ",num[j]);
    }
    getch();
}
```

Lab 1 | 1.10

OUTPUT

Enter the 5 number:

23 43 56 12 34

Numbers in ascending order:

12 23 34 43 56

5. Write a C program to Calculate the sum of all numbers from 0 to 100 (both inclusive) that are divisible by 4

Program:

```c
#include<stdio.h>
#include<conio.h>

void main()
{
int sum=0,rem,i;
clrscr();
printf("Sum of no.from 0 to 100 that are divisible by 4 :");
   for(i=0;i<=100;i++)
        {
rem=i%4;
if(rem==0)
sum=sum+i;
        }
        printf("%d",sum);
        getch();
}
```

OUTPUT

Sum of the no.from 0 to 100 that are divisible by 4 : 1300

6. Write a program to accept length of three sides of tringle and to test and print the type of tringle – equilateral, isosceles, right angle, none of these.

```c
#include<stdio.h>
#include<conio.h>
#include<math.h>

void main()
{
 int a, b, c;
 clrscr();
 printf("Enter the values of the sides of the triangle: \n");
 scanf("%d %d %d", &a, &b, &c);
  if (a == b && b == c)
  {
   printf("Equilateral Triangle. \n");
  }

  else if (a == b || b == c || a == c)
  {
   printf("Isosceles Triangle. \n");
  }
  else if((a*a==b*b+c*c) || (b*b==a*a+c*c) || (c*c==b*b+a*a))

   printf("Rightangle Triangle. \n");
  else
   printf("None of these \n");
 getch();
 }
```

OUTPUT

Enter the values of the sides of the triangle:

14 14 14

Equilateral Triangle.

7. Write a program to accept a string from console and display the following.

(a) Total number of character in string

(b) Total number of vowels in string

(c) Total number of occurrence of character 'a' in string

(d) Total number of occurrence of string 'the' in string

```
#include<stdio.h>
#include<conio.h>
void main()
{
  int i,n,c=0,v=0,a=0,the=0;
  char str[30];
  printf("enter a string");
  gets(str);
  for(i=0;str[i]!='\0';i++)
  {
    c++;

if(str[i]=='a'||str[i]=='e'||str[i]=='i'||str[i]=='o'||str[i]=='u')
    v++;
    if(str[i]=='a')
    a++;
    if(str[i]=='t'&&str[i+1]=='h'&&str[i+2]=='e')
    the++;
  }
  printf("\n lenght of string is %d",c);
  printf("\n total number of vowels are %d",v);
  printf("\n total number of accurence of character a is %d",a);
  printf("\n total number of times string the accour in given string is %d",the);
  getch();
}
```

OUTPUT

enter a string

the roshan

lenght of string is 10

total number of vowels are 3

total number of accurence of character a is 1

total number of times string the accour in given string is 1

8. Write a class to convert character string of lower case to uppercase and numeric digit in reverse order.

```
#include<stdio.h>
#include<conio.h>

void main()
{
    int num,newnum=0,rem=0;
    clrscr();
    printf("\nTake the number to reverse:");
    scanf("%d",&num);

    while(num>0)
    {
        rem=num%10;
        newnum=(newnum*10)+rem;
    }
    printf("\nReverse number=%d",newnum);
    getch();
```

OUTPUT

Take the number to reverse:

214

Reverse number= 412

9. Write a program in C to read an integer and display each of the digit of integer in English.

```c
#include<stdio.h>
#include<conio.h>
#include<math.h>
void main()
{
    int num, newnum=0,rem;
    clrscr();
    printf("\nenter the number::");
    scanf("%d",&num);
    while(num>0)
    {
        rem=num%10;
        newnum=(newnum*10)+rem;
        num=num/10;
    }
    while(newnum>0)
    {
        rem=newnum%10;
        switch(rem)
            case 0:printf("zero");
                   break;
            case 1:printf("One");
                   break;
            case 2:printf("two");
                   break;
            case 3:printf("three");
                   break;
            case 4:printf("four");
                   break;
            case 5:printf("five");
                   break;
            case 6:printf("six");
                   break;
            case 7:printf("seven");
                   break;
            case 8:printf("eight");
```

```
                    break;
            case 9:printf("nine");
                    break;
        }
        newnum=newnum/10;
    }
    getch();
}
```

OUTPUT

enter the number::

214

two one four

10. Write a program to generate first 20 Fibonacci series.

```
#include<stdio.h>
#include<conio.h>
void main()
//main starts
{
int pev=0,next=1,i=0,sum,length;
//initialisation
    clrscr();
//clear screen
    printf("\nEnter the length of fiboseries::");
//input
    scanf("%d",&length);
    printf("\n%d",prev); //first member of series
    do
        {       //logic of do while loop
        sum=prev+next;
        printf("\n%d",sum);   //printing output
```

```
            prev=next;
            next=sum;
            i++;
        }while(i<length);
        getch();
    }
```

OUTPUT

Enter the length of fibo series::20
```
    0
    1
    2
    3
    5
    8
    13
    21
    34
    55
    89
    144
    233
    377
    610
    987
    1597
    2584
    4181
    6765
    10946
```

11. Write a program to generate prime number between 1 to n.

```c
#include<stdio.h>
#include<conio.h>
void main()
{
 int i,n;
 printf("enter a number");
 scanf("%d",&n);
 for(i=2;i<=n;i++)
 {

if(i%2!=0&&i%3!=0&&i%4!=0&&i%5!=0&&i%6!=0&&i%7!=0&&i%8!=0&&i%9!=0)
  printf("\n %d",i);
 }
 getch();
 }
```

OUTPUT

enter a number

20

11

13

17

19

10. Write a program to compute GCD of given two integer.

FPL – I ENGG. (F.E. SEM. I)   ASSIGNMENTS

```
#include<stdio.h>
#include<conio.h>

void main(){

    int x,y,m,i;

    printf("Insert any two number: ");

    scanf("%d%d",&x,&y);
    if(x>y)
            m=y;
    else
            m=x;

    for(i=m;i>=1;i--){
        if(x%i==0&&y%i==0){
            printf("\n GCD of two number is %d",i; break;
        }
    }
    getch();
}
```

OUTPUT

Insert any two number:
20 30
GCD of two number is : 10

13. Write a program in C to compute factorial of given positive integer using recursive function.

```c
#include<stdio.h>
int fact(int);
void main()
{
   int num,f;
   printf("\n Enter a number: ");
   scanf("%d",&num);
   f=fact(num);
   printf("\nFactorial of %d is: %d",num,f);
   getch();
}

int fact(int n)
{
   if(n==1)
       return 1;
   else
       return(n*fact(n-1));
}
```

OUTPUT

Enter a number: 5

Factorial of 5 is: 120

Enter the length of

---

14. Write a program in C to compute roots of quadratic equation.

```c
#include <stdio.h>
#include <conio.h>
#include<math.h>
void main()
{
   int a,b,c,d;/* d is a discriminent */
   float x1,x2;/* here x1 is root1 and x2 is root2*/
   printf("enter the value of a,b & c\n");
   scanf("%d%d%d",&a,&b,&c);
```

FPL – I ENGG. (F.E. SEM. I)   ASSIGNMENTS

```c
        d=b*b-4*a*c;
        if(d==0)
        {
          printf("Both roots are equal\n");
          x1=-b/(2*a);
          x2=x1;
          printf("First  Root x1= %f\n",x1);
          printf("Second Root x2= %f\n",x2);
        }
        else
        if(d>0)
        {
        printf("Both roots are real and different\n");
        x1=(-b+sqrt(d))/(2*a);
        x2=(-b-sqrt(d))/(2*a);
        printf("First  Root x1= %f\n",x1);
        printf("Second Root x2= %f\n",x2);
        }
        else
            {
          printf("Root are imeginary\n No Solution \n");
          x1=sqrt(-d)/ (2.0*a)
                x2=-x1
                printf("First  Root x1= %f\n",x1);
          printf("Second Root x2= %f\n",x2);
            }
            getch();
}
```

OUTPUT

enter the value of a,b & c 6

  -13

   6

Both roots are real and different

First Root x1= 1.500000

First Root x1= 0.666667

15. Write a program to sort integer using bubble sort.

```c
#include<stdio.h>
#include<conio.h>
void main()
{
   int a[5],i,j,temp;
   clrscr();
   printf("\nEnter the elements to sort::");
   for(i=0;i<5;i++)
   scanf("%d",&a[i]);
   for(i=0;i<5;i++)
     {
        for(j=i+1;j<5;j++)
        {
     if(a[i]>a[j])
       {
          temp=a[i];
          a[i]=a[j];
          a[j]=temp;
        }
      }
    }
    printf("\n\nSorted list::");
    for(i=0;i<5;i++)
    printf("\t%d",a[i]);
    getch();
}
```

OUTPUT

Enter the elements to sort::45 0 137 15 12

Sorted list::   0   12   15   45   137

16. Write a program to compute addition / substraction / multiplication of two matrices. Use function to add/subtract/multiply two matrices.

```c
#include<stdio.h>
#include<conio.h>
void main()
{
int i,j,opt,k;
int x[3][3],y[3][3],z[3][3];
clrscr();
printf("\n\tEnter The Value Of First Matrix:");
    for(i=1;i<=3;i++)
    {
        for(j=1;j<=3;j++)
        {
        scanf("%d",&x[i][j]);
        }
    }
printf("\nEnter The Value Of Second Matrix:");
    for(i=1;i<=3;i++)
    {
        for(j=1;j<=3;j++)
        {
        scanf("%d",&y[i][j]);
        }
    }
do {
printf("\nSelect One Option given below:\n");
printf("\n\t1.ADDITION");
printf("\n\t2.SUBTRACTION");
printf("\n\t3.MULTIPICATION");
printf("\n\t4.Exit");
printf("\n\tEnter Your option:");
scanf("%d",&opt);
switch(opt)
```

```c
{
   case 1:for(i=1;i<=3;i++)
      {
      for(j=1;j<=3;j++)
         {
         z[i][j]=x[i][j]+y[i][j];
         printf("\t %d",z[i][j]);
         }
      printf("\n");
      }
      break;
   case 2:
      for(i=1;i<=3;i++)
   {
      for(j=1;j<=3;j++)
      {
      z[i][j]=x[i][j]-y[i][j];
      printf("\t %d",z[i][j]);
      }
      printf("\n");
   }
      break;
   case 3:
      for(i=1;i<=3;i++)
      {
         for(j=1;j<=3;j++)
         {
         z[i][j]=0;
         for(k=1;k<=3;k++)
         z[i][j]=x[i][k]*y[k][j]+z[i][j];
         printf("\t %d",z[i][j]);
         }
      }
      printf("\n");
```

```
        }
        break;
    case 4:
        exit(0);
        break;
    }
}while(opt<5);
    getch();
}
```

OUTPUT

Enter The Value Of First Matrix:

Sorted list::   0   12   15   45   137

17. Write a program to carry out following operation on the string by using library function accept a string from console and display the following.

(a) To concatenate String S2 to string S1

(b) To find length of given string

(c) To compare two string S1 and S2

(d) To copy string S2 to another string S1

```
#include<stdio.h>
#include<conio.h>
#include<string.h>
void main()
{
char s1[10],s2[20],s3[10],s4[10];
int n;
clrscr();
printf("\n\nEnter the String to calculate length::");
scanf("%s",s1);
n=strlen(s1);
printf("\n\nLength of entered string is
```

```
:%d\n",n);
strcpy(s2,s1);
printf("\nthe copied string is :%s\n",s2);
printf("\n Enter the string to concatenate::");
scanf("%s",s3);
strcat(s2,s3);
printf("\nThe concatenated string is:%s\n",s2);
printf("\nEnter the string to compare::");
scanf("%s",s4);
  if(!strcmp(s4,s2))
    {
       printf("\nString are equal");
    }
   else
     {
        printf("\nstring are not equal");
     }
   getch();
 }
```

OUTPUT

Enter the String to calculate length: Champ

Length of entered string is :5

the copied string is :Champ

Enter the string to concatenate:: Roshan

The concatenated string is:ChampRoshan

Enter the string to compare::Quit

string are not equal

Notes

Notes

www.ingramcontent.com/pod-product-compliance
Lightning Source LLC
Chambersburg PA
CBHW062133160426
43191CB00013B/2294